To: LEDELLE

THANK YOU FOR YOUR SUPPORT

GOD BLESS YOU.

3. 2015

To: LEDELLE

THANK You For your support

GOD Bless You.

3. 2015

MORE THAN MOTOWN

MORE THAN MOTOWN

THE JEROME EWING STORY BOOK ONE

JEROME EWING

To order additional copies of this book, contact:
Xlibris
1-888-795-4274
www.Xlibris.com
Orders@Xlibris.com
651140

CONTENTS

HE'S COOL LIKE LL cool J

AND HE'S COLD AS ICE CUBE

HE'S BAD LIKE MICHAEL

JACKSON

AND HE'S FRESH LIKE PRINCE

OF BEL-AIR

HE'S THE CREAM OF THE CROP LIKE

EDDIE

KENDRICKS

HE'S MOTOWN, HE'S STAX, HE'S MCA, HE'S SO SO DEF, HE'S CBS/SONY

HE'S A BALLER

HE'S A BOXER

HE'S **JEROME**

ONE OF AMERICA'S MOST FORTUNATE PHOTOGRAPHERS, JEROME HAS BEEN THE MAN AT THE RIGHT PLACE AT THE RIGHT TIME ON MANY OCCASIONS.

HE'S BEEN TO THE NBA DRAFT,

HE'S BEEN WITH THE REAL DEAL,

HE'S BEEN WITH THE REAL MCCOY

HE'S BEEN WITH THE PIPED PIPER OF SOUL

BOBBY WOMACK **AND**

THE BAD BOY OF ENTERTAINMENT, BOBBY

BROWN,  **HE'S BEEN IN THE PURPLE RAIN WITH PRINCE**

  **AND ON**

THE MIDNIGHT TRAIN TO GEORGIA WITH

GLADYS KNIGHT

HE'S BEEN CHASING WATERFALLS WITH TLC,

HE'S A SMOOTH OPERATOR LIKE SADE

HE'S JEROME

ASK MARTIN LAWRENCE OR

THE TIME  He's

Jerome

NOW ASK YOURSELF, WHO WILL HAVE THE HOTTEST BOOK OF THE YEAR?

Imagine going on a journey where you meet and hang out with some of the world's most influential people. *More than Motown* is a fast-paced story with a guest list that includes Prince, Michael Jackson, Stevie Wonder, Russell Simmons, Bobby Womack, Luther Vandross, Jay-Z, P. Diddy, Usher, TLC, Sade, R. Kelly, Evander Holyfield, Bobby Brown, and Whitney Houston. You will hear stories about singers, actors, politicians, and sports icons.

This book will quickly become one of your favorites. As it takes you on the other side of the camera, you will see the ups and downs of the life of the people that make the people who are in front of the camera. Filled with never-before seen pictures, entertainment and personal stories shared by first time author Jerome Ewing.

Jerome Ewing has lived his life like the Undercover Boss. The secret to his success has unfolded like magic as he was catapulted right into a career of Photography. Jerome worked with most major record labels. Motown Records, MCA, Arista, CBS, Mercury Records, So So Def, Jive Records, among others.

It's no wonder Jerome ended up capturing pictures of movie stars. "The right man, in the right place, at the right time." Jerome has constantly ended up in the presence of R&B Moguls. He was a regular with them even prior to them becoming famous. Nobody knows what really goes on backstage like the unassuming photographer. He stands quietly by and takes pictures. After you read Jerome's exciting book, you will understand from a bird's eye glimpse of all the backstage drama as unfolds from a photographer's view.

Jerome has been jolted into a lifestyle of backstage photography from some of the most unsuspected individuals especially the rich and famous! Once you read his book you will ask "How in the world did he get in there?" Believe this; there is an explanation.

Jerome was born in Chicago Illinois and at early age his family moved to Memphis TN. He attended Lemoyne Owens College where he studied Photography with no idea of where this occupation would lead him. He was literally fascinated by the magical concept of photography and immediately developed a homemade personal photography lab that eventually led him on a miraculous journey to Atlanta Georgia.

This Moving story "More than Motown" will swell your heart with pride, joy and laughter as you explore these fresh and unpredictable stories about Jerome's exploitation of his backstage journey of some of the biggest shows of all times.

If you enjoy reading fresh, exciting, changeable, invigorating and exhilarating yet humorous stories; this indeed is the book for you!

More Than Motown: The Jerome Ewing Story. The Autobiography of Photographer Jerome Ewing.

 **Gladys Knight / Jerome Ewing**

Intro

Welcome to my world. This truly is a story about how I was blessed beyond my imagination, how I had a chance to live a fantasy life, make plenty of money, and build a photographer's dream portfolio. In my first book my intention was to start this story, about what happen to me in 1977. However, after talking with other writers, I was convinced that people would be interested in reading about my background and what it took for me to get to where I am today. My good friend William Bedford, who is a former NBA player with Phoenix, Detroit, and San Antonio, told me that when he was writing his book, people wanted to know about his struggles, his background, and his family life. He said that those were the things that make someone unique. Well, that made a lot of sense to me because I started with nothing. I was born into a poor family that was from Chicago, Illinois. My family never settled anywhere for a long time until we moved to Memphis, Tennessee, in the late '70s. My mother lived in that little house in Memphis, Tennessee, for more than thirty-five years until her untimely death in 2011. I started putting this book together in 2012.

I still live in Memphis, Tennessee, but I am looking at other options, including getting married again. My main reason for writing this book is the journey that God has taken me on, the people I met along the way, and the parts of history that I was able to record along the way. I used to say that I was lucky to have an opportunity to achieve such a task. Nevertheless, I now say that all this has been a blessing to me. My path has been orchestrated by God Almighty. God's hands were all over me. God has never left me, and for that reason, I praise his name! I believe that writing this book is one way of sharing God's holy words with the world and to inspire someone else to seek their dream through the power of his glory!

Jerome Ewing

The Chicago Years

I was born in Chicago, Illinois, on August 24, 1957. I was the second child out of four children. My older brother's name was Lynell, my sister's name is Jeanine, and my youngest brother's name is Edward. My mother's name was Vestine, and my father's name was Edward Sr. Growing up in Chicago was good in the early '60s. My first memory was when John F. Kennedy was killed. I had to be about six years old. I remember one of my teachers that I had a crush on telling the whole class to sit on the floor near her desk, and I noticed that some of the other teachers were crying. I didn't understand what was going on, but I could tell that it wasn't something good. I believe that we got out of school early that day. I lived right across the street from Medill Elementary School, so I didn't have very far to walk.

By time that I made it to the sixth grade, I thought I was the fastest kid alive. We used to play a game called rush during recess time. One person would stand in the middle of the playground, and everybody would line up and spread across the fence. The person in the middle would then yell, "Rush!" and everybody else would run toward him. If he touched you, then you would stay out there. So more and more people would be in the middle until the last person was left. Guess who the last person was 95 percent of the time? Your boy! That game of rush was an important part of my early years because everybody in school knew who I was. Everybody wanted to be my friend. Since I lived across the street from the school, it made me feel it was my school and I actually owned the school. Now the place where I lived was called the Village. This was a row of houses that had units. Each unit had an upstairs and downstairs compartments. There were about eight units per building. After I mastered the game of rush, I felt that I needed something else to do. I would watch the Chicago Cubs play baseball because WGN was the only TV station that our little black-and-white TV would pick up. As I watched the games, I started to play games that were similar to baseball. The year of 1967 on Christmas, I receive my first baseball glove.

By the summer of 1968, I could throw a ball so far in the air on one side of the row houses and run around on the other side and catch it. Now I really thought I was the shit. Back in those days, your neighbors were your best friends. In fact, when my mother passed away in 2011, one of her friends came by the house and stated that the world had changed. Nowadays, most people don't even want to know their neighbors. Back in the day, when a person was still young, there were so many things that he just didn't know. I didn't know that I was poor. I didn't know that we were black. I didn't know that the people around us weren't going to be there forever. I didn't know people who died would ever come back. All these things came into reality later in my life.

By the end of summer, my mother and father had a fight. I found out later that

my father was an alcoholic. My mother put him out of our house. Then a few months later, my mother moved our family from the Village to the Jane Addams. Those two projects were only a few miles apart. My grandmother already lived in the Jane Addams. Lucky for us, we moved into the same building. It was great how my grandmother took care of us. My mother was admitted to the hospital and diagnosed with tuberculosis. Later, the state sent a nanny to take care of us. I was afraid of our nanny, because we never been exposed

to being cared for by anyone other than my mother and my grandmother. Further, our nanny walked with a limp and wore too much makeup. She smelled funny, and I didn't want her to touch me. So my grandmother stepped in, and again she started taking care of us. We used to go over to her house, and she would make us a pallet to sleep on, and she had a balcony on the third floor. So when we moved to the second floor, I felt like I was in heaven.

Not long after moving into the Jane Addams and everything was going very well, we started going to a new school called Jacob A. Riis. It was only 150 feet from our house. We got lucky again, and a place that would change my life was at our back door called Old Town Chicago Boys' Club. The playground was right outside our front door, and there was a store right across the street. That was something we never had in the village. I was about to get another dose of reality. Dr. Martin Luther King was assassinated. "Black people, black people, black people." That was all I would hear around that time. There were many riots in my own neighborhood. They tore down their own stores in the neighborhood. That was the reality that made me realize that I was black and what Martin Luther King was doing, and now he was dead and was not coming back. I started to understand what the Black Panther Party and the West Side Organization (I first meet Jesse Jackson when I was a little boy). I was only ten years of age, and the world had gone haywire. I tried to block out as much as I could, but shortly afterward, my oldest brother was drafted into a gang. I had mixed emotions about it, but he later told me that if he didn't join the gang, we would have a lot of problems. Therefore, he said that he had to handle it and there was not much that he could do about it. Instead of me joined the gang with my older brother Pouch. I joined Old Town Boys' Club on the corner of Taylor Street and South Racine. I became the Boy of the Year, in 1971. My picture was in the newspaper with an actor named Forrest Tucker from a TV show called *F Troop*. I had a chance to meet Bob Love of the Chicago Bulls; I won trophies for baseball, softball, table tennis, high jump, four-by-four relay, and bumper pool and was a two-time MVP in softball. All things were going well for me. I don't brag, but if you have ever seen the catch that Willie Mays made over his head and spin and throw it back into the infield all in one motion, you would say it was a great catch. I would make catches like that every day. I was able to hit the baseball at four hundred feet when I was only fifteen or sixteen years old. I could pitch and play third base and second base, as well as catch if I needed to catch. Most coaches wanted me to play outfield or pitch. I remember a new show called *Red Hot and Blue* came on; it later became *Soul Train*. It was on a channel on UHF or something like that. Then they got a big budget and moved to Los Angeles. It was a dance show, and I wanted go on the show, but my grades were too low, so I went to Crane High School for summer. On the first day of school, some thugs made us line up against the wall to rob us. I didn't have much money, so it didn't bother me that much. They took some people's new shoe and all our money, and I never got a chance to be on the show, because I didn't go back. But all was well until my grandmother passed away.

This happened back in 1972. That was one of the hardest things that I have ever encountered in my life. My grandmother always took care of us. She always saw to it that we were fed. She also beat my ass a couple times. Her death was a big blow to me! Within months, we were packing again and leaving Chicago for good. I realized that life is not always fair, when one door closes, another one opens. My mother was doing the best she could. Everything she did was to make it better for all of us.

I was in high school, looking forward in playing baseball. I was in love (puppy Love) at the time. I had lots of friends, cousins whom I loved dearly. I always enjoyed spending the nights over their house.

The Hopkins Park Years

In 1973, I went from city boy to country boy. We moved to Hopkins Park, Illinois, with my uncle. He raised horses for people who lived in Chicago. They would come out on the weekend to ride their horses.

Imagine leaving a big city like Chicago and ending up in a poor small country town like Hopkins Park, Illinois. As I said earlier, I didn't know that we were poor. I thought that everybody lived the same way. By the time I got to Hopkins Park, I was now sixteen years old. My baseball dreams were shattered. Now I was looking at dirt roads, no street-lights and it got extremely dark in the country. But my mama was very happy! She was with her brother, I wasn't a selfish kid. I was getting used to moving and making new friends. I was thinking they were about to see the greatest baseball player they had ever seen. There had to be some pretty girls there. My uncle was one of the people lived there that had money. He worked at a rock quarry for more than twenty years. He had houses, cars, trucks, and land, and everybody knew him. He was married, and they had three girls. When they told me about the school that I would be going to, I got even happier. The name of the school was Saint Anne High School. The star basketball player's name was Jack Sikma. He graduated (the year before I got there) and later went on to the NBA with the Seattle Supersonics. I was now thinking that I could really play some baseball and that I would get drafted by the Chicago Cubs or the White Sox. Well, a funny thing happened on the way to the forum. At that time, I was only sixteen years of age, and I was prone to making some mistakes, and this was where I made one of the biggest mistakes of my life. That mistake still bothers me even to this day. I should have asked for help, I had gone through so much and I thought I was so smart. I had a chip on my shoulder. We had to ride a bus to school, and that was different for me. What happened was, I was told that the school was twenty miles from Hopkins Park. I always ended up living right by the school within walking distance, but now if you missed the bus, you wouldn't get to go to school unless you had backup transportation like a car or something. Our bus came at 7:00 a.m. We had to make a lot of stops, so we would have to be up at 6:00 a.m., because things were different while living with my uncle. He had three children, and there were four of us, and everybody had to get to the bathroom. The lights were turned out at about nine every night so that we could get up on time. We had a long thirty to forty minutes' ride, and sometimes when we arrived at school, it was not always a great day. There thing in life I had to learned to accept.

In 1973, I was only five years old after the death of Dr. Martin Luther King, not every teacher at the school was very friendly. The town of Saint Anne was mostly white, and we were being bused to their school. Black and white students were really trying hard to get along at that time. Then here I come, a pretty boy from the city with a chip on my shoulder, I had a few fights. I heard some racial slurs, but I was determined to make the best of it. September was basketball season, and baseball tryouts were offered in January and February. I thought, *Cool.* I was looking good in my physical education class. I was thinking I was not going to let no white boys out do me in anything. I decided to go out for the basketball team. Now here where I could have used the advice that Michael Jordan got, I did just the opposite. This all happened back in 1973. I stayed after school to try out for the basketball team; the coach (an older white male) was also the baseball coach. He timed us with his stopwatch while we were running. I was fast, really fast, and I knew that he had seen me playing basketball in PE. Here I was, the new kid on the block, and I was from Chicago, so I felt pretty good about my chances, but a funny thing happened on my way to the forum. I thought that I had an okay first day. However, I missed a few shots and some lay- up, but was great on defense. I knew that I could use some polishing up, but so could most of the other kids that were trying out for the team. I left there that day thinking that at least I wasn't the worst player there.

But the next day at school, I was one of the first students cut from the team. To tell you the truth, I was hurt both inside and out. I didn't know what to say because I had been bragging on the bus. The coach didn't cut some of the people that I thought that I had outplayed. I also noticed that all those guys were white, and that was all I could come up with on that. Then I came up with my dumb-ass plan. I was not going to try out for baseball, and it was going to be his loss because I was good at baseball. *I could play that game in my sleep*, I thought. I was fast, and he would regret cutting me. It took me years, maybe five or six years, to realize that I played myself. How stupid was that! He kept coaching, and I did not get a scholarship, and I was the one looking like the fool. The thing about it was, I should have played baseball and made a name for myself. And then I should've gone back the following year and tried out for basketball. I think things would've been a lot different for me. I believe that was an opportunity to change people's minds. Instead, I carried an attitude around the school campus, which didn't help anybody. By 1975, I couldn't waited to graduate and get out of that school, and as of today, I've never gone back. Now I understand how stupid I was. I might go back someday and reminisce what I could have been. As my time at Saint Anne High

School was coming to a close, so was my time in Hopkins Park. We had Moved from my uncle's house early that year and moved into a double-sided trailer house. From the first day in the trailer house, I knew that we would not stay there. It was new, and it was nice. It was better than a lot of the houses around us, but it was in a field in a curve. On windy days, the trailer would shake really bad. We knew that if a big storm came along, the trailer would be blown away.

That last year at Hopkins Park wasn't bad at all. In fact, for me it was great! One day I came home from school, they were clearing away some trees, and before you knew it, a new trailer was next door. Our new neighbor was a twenty-five-year-old single female. Let me tell you, when a single female moves into a neighborhood, most men, single or not, know she is single. She would always stop or drive slow if she saw me, and she would wave.

One day I didn't go to school. I think I had sprained my ankle. I was sitting on my front steps, smoking. The lady next door came out of her house looking as if she was searching for something. She saw me and waved, and I went back into the house. Within minutes, I heard someone blowing their horn. She pulled up in my drive-way. I went out to talk to her. She wanted to know why I was home that day. After thinking a few minutes, she let me know that she was going to the store and asked if I needed anything. Now put yourself in my position. What would you have done? My answer was "What do you mean?"

"What can I get for you to make you feel better?" she said.

I laughed for a minute, and then I told her what I wanted wasn't at the store. When I told her that, she wanted to know where my mother was. I told her that everybody was gone.

"I'm by myself," I said.

All of a sudden, she changed her mind about going to the store. I locked the door and met her at her house, and it was on. For the next few months, she made sure I had what I needed. Then one day, she took me to Kankakee, Illinois, and bought me a Cadillac. That blew my mind. My mother had mixed emotions about all that. Within a month, I graduated and moved to Kankakee, Illinois. Now I didn't think it had anything to do with her. My mom met a man and moved in with him. He sold houses, so we had a house, and I had a car, and everybody was calling me a player. My nickname was Macaroni, taken from the Richard Pryor *That Nigger's Crazy* album, and that's what I'm still known as in Kankakee.

Since my uncle and cousins were still in Hopkins Park, which is about twenty miles from Kankakee, we would spend more time in Hopkins Park than in Kankakee. All our new friends were out there, and I had someone out there who lived by herself and was good to me. My thing was that I was tired of moving. Whatever my mother wanted to do, I was going to do it. She always asked first, and we always said, "Whatever you want to do." I wish I had simply said no to my mother.

The Kankakee Years

By this time in my life, I never had a steady girlfriend. That could've been due in part to my remembering a babysitter that I once had, who would wake me up in the middle of the night to show her friends my eyes.

My eyes used to change colors, and people would stare at me, and somehow that caused me to be shy. I used to play ball all day so that I wouldn't be around girls. Then when I did find girls, my family would move. I didn't go to the prom because the girl that bought me a car was too old for me to take her to the prom. I didn't want my friends or other people to see me with her.

One day I went to a summer festival in Momence, Illinois, it was very nice. There were lots of women there. All I saw were women in shorts and halter tops. Damn, there were some good-looking women there. I was with my partner, Fonz. I ended up meeting a girl and her name was Angie. She had ass, tits, and good hair, and she was very pretty. She lived in Hopkins Park, and we started dating. Her mother was crazy about me, her brother and sister also were happy to see us together.

Back in those days, we had a house phone, we would be on the phone for hours while talking about nothing. Now that I had a car I could pick up Angie. We would hang out for hours. We would go to lovers' lane, drive-in movies the woods and anywhere else we decided to go. For the first time in my life, I stayed in a relationship. My sister's boyfriend got himself a house in Hopkins Park, and my sister moved in with him. Later, I obtained a job with CETA, which is a government program, and I was now receiving a check. About the same time all this good stuff was happening in my life. My mother was experiencing problems with the man she had moved to Kankakee with and she knew this guy was going to be a problem. She was ready to leave him and move again.

However, doors were opening for me, and doors were closing for her. By this time my oldest brother Lynell, had gotten a girl pregnant. Neither one of them had a job, so he started hanging out with the wrong people, just to make some money. Sometimes I would go in his room, and he would have a whole shoe box of weed, and he would be bagging it up. If my mother had caught him in her house with that stuff, she would have kicked his ass. My brother Edward was rolling with the punches. Nevertheless, I started to feel like something was about to happen. I mean, I just didn't feel like these situations would continue to last for a long time, and I was right.

When we left Chicago, my aunt Lenora, my mother's oldest sister, also left Chicago. My Aunt Lenora was in a bad accident, the bus she was riding on flipped over and she was broken up pretty bad. When she received her settlement, she was a blessing to my mother and she had plenty left. When we moved to Hopkins Park, My aunt bought a trailer and put it on my uncle's land, she was very happy. My aunt's back was not healing very well. She was actually getting worse. That told her that the cold weather was going to be bad for her and that she needed to move to a warmer climate. And since we had relatives in Phoenix and in Memphis, my aunt decided to move to Phoenix. While she was deciding on what she was going to do, I got my own news. Angie was pregnant, and my sister had found out that she was pregnant all in one month. My mother moved back to Hopkins Park with my aunt, and they decided together that they would eventually move to Phoenix. Things became very crazy in my life at that time. I was playing baseball on a team in Kankakee, so I could go to Kankakee Community College. I was doing very well at that time. This was therapy for me. My summer job had expired, and I was able to obtain a job at a furniture plant, I had gotten myself a house, and Angie moved in with me. In the meantime, my sister and her boyfriend were raided by drug enforcement, and her boyfriend was arrested.

My mother and Aunt Lenora were preparing to move to Phoenix, and now my pregnant sister had to go with them. So within weeks, my pregnant sister and my youngest brother, along with my mother and aunt, all took off to Phoenix. My brother Lynell and I stayed in Kankakee. This was very emotional for me. This was the first time that my mother had moved and I didn't move with her. I was now on my own. My sister couldn't stay. There was no way that she was going to allow Jeanine to stay with us, because she didn't know if her boyfriend was going to get out of jail or not.

I was nineteen years old, and Lynell was twenty. So I felt that we could handle whatever came our way. We were tight. He had looked out for me all my life, so I was cool. Well, after they all left, things started to change again. First, the furniture plant laid off workers, and since I was new, I was laid off. We were out of work, but the office that hired me for the plant job allowed me to enter into another program. I was assigned to work for a guy who owned lots of houses and apartments. I was cool for about a month, and then the house that we were living in was purchased by another company who wanted to tear down the houses so that they could build some new apartments.

My love for Kankakee started to shrink. They moved me into some ghetto apartments. Then one day while watching TV, I heard a lot of noise outside my window. When I went to the window and looked out, I heard a woman saying "Don't kill him, don't kill him!" Man, there were about thirty people watching these two brothers beating the hell out of this boy with chains. They were stomping him, kicking him, and hitting him with those chains. Those boys had just gotten out of jail, and the boy that they were beating was over his girlfriend's house. She was also pleading with them to stop, and nobody would help. Here I was, new in this building, and I felt bad that I couldn't stop them. However, who was going to stop them from turning on me? When the police and ambulance arrived, they turned him over, his head was swollen. I didn't know why this had happened to him, but I did know that I didn't want to live around that kind of shit. Angie wouldn't stay over there, and after she got her welfare check and food stamps, she moved out and got her own house somewhere else.

Eventually, I moved away from that crazy-ass apartment and moved in with Angie, we were cool for a few months. Then her sister moved across the street, and for some reason, Angie and I started having fights every day. At the same time, Angie's mother moved from Hopkins Park to Saint Louis. Her sister wanted to go where their mother lived. So we decided to go our separate ways. Angie went to Saint Louis, and I went to Memphis. You might wonder why Memphis and not Phoenix. Well, it was like this, "A funny thing happened on the way to the forum."

Now I knew that it was time for me to leave Kankakee when I got fired from my job. My boss said that the men in the apartments where I was working didn't like me being in their houses while they were at work. I never messed with any of them, but I was called Macaroni, so I understood; I needed money so that I could leave. My brother moved in one of my mother's boyfriend's houses. Then I found out that he was also selling weed for him. My mother didn't know that my brother was selling drugs for her ex-boyfriend, but she did know he was the big man in town. I told my brother that we were going to get our asses out of there. I was eating from the money that I made at baseball practice. I would tell everybody to put up two dollars each, and whoever got the most hits got the money. I won the money every day, until they just stopped putting up money for that. I was a natural-born hustler. I had sold my car to eat. Now I needed a car. I went to an auction and bought a lot of stuff, I sold it for double the money. Then I bought a car from my girlfriend's sister's boyfriend. The only thing that was wrong with the car it needed brakes. I did the craziest thing to get money to repair the brakes. I asked a friend named Elmore to ride to Chicago with me I told him that I was going down to Jew Town (Maxwell Street) and back to (Kankakee). Now Elmore was a pimp or player type, just a cool dude, and he had lots of ladies. I met him through my sister's boyfriend that was in jail. He agreed to go with me. He was going to Jew Town to buy some shoes or something. Anyway, the only thing I didn't tell him was that my car didn't have brakes. I had already put the gas in my car, so I didn't have to stop. So I jumped right on 57 North, and we were jamming. I had a strap under my seat. We were fine for a while, clear sailing, and there was no traffic. The closer we got to Chicago, I had to start hitting on the brakes, they were grinding very hard. Then we hit a traffic jam that was bumper to bumper. I couldn't stop! I had to jump out on the shoulder, and he started to scream, "Man, what the f——k, you ain't got no brakes!"

"I didn't know that they were that bad," I replied. I was weaving in and out of traffic.

He was so mad at me when we got to Jew Town. He was saying, "You can drop me off at the bus station."

I told him that I was sorry and that we would be all right. I told him to get what we need and get back to the highway before traffic got too bad. He looked at me with tears in his eyes and said, "Man, you are a damn fool." We argued for a while, said a prayer, and got the hell out of there. We made it back safe. Elmore jumped out of my car mad as hell, and I never saw him again (sorry, brother). I got my brakes fixed with the money that I made.

My brother went to see his baby, and we went to Hopkins Park to say our good-byes. Then we came back to Kankakee to see Angie and my baby. Then we loaded up all we could load, and then we hit the road. Next, I called my mother. She had stopped in Memphis to see her uncle, my grandmother's brother. He talked them into staying there before going to Phoenix. My sister was now nine months pregnant, and she was due anytime. If they were going to make it to Phoenix, they better go now. So they decided not to take that chance. The lady next door to my uncle had just moved, and my uncle knew the landlord, so they moved my mother next door to him, which was right across the street from South Side High School.

The Memphis Years (Round 1)

Lynell and I were taking our time riding to Memphis until we went through Arkansas. I pulled over at a gas station and got some gas and munchies. Lynell decided that he was going to drive on from that point. I was cool with that, and in about twenty minutes into driving, we saw the blue lights flashing, and we were being pulled over. I didn't think that he was speeding; however, the cop was much less than friendly. Since it was our first time in the South, we took that ticket and got the hell out of there. They took his license, and he never went back to get them, and he never had licenses while living in Memphis.

Lynell always had problems, because most people wanted to see his driver's license. I really hated that happened, because I think it changed his future in Memphis. Every job that he got, he had to walk or catch a ride. He worked for a paint company. Some of the people that worked there died from a brain tumor, including my brother. Someday, I will have someone to look into that. Anyway, when we made it to Memphis, I would say that it didn't start off too good. My mother got a job across the street, at South Side High School in the lunchroom with my aunt next door. She left a key under the mat and a note on the stove. So Lynell went next door over my uncle's house with my cousin James. I found a pizza in the freezer, so I put it in the oven while I was in the restroom, and I thought that it was cooking. It was still frozen, so I turned the oven off, picked up the note, and read it again, and it said, "You have to light the oven at the bottom." Then I turned the gas back on, took my lighter out of my pocket, and bent down to light it, and all I heard was *fofo*. Man, all my hair was gone—my mustache, my eyebrows, and my eyelashes were all burned off instantly!

I turned that oven off immediately and got some Vaseline and put it on my face. My brother and my sister came home that day laughing at me. Man, that shit hurt. It wasn't funny to my mother at first, and then she got in on the fun later. Then we realized that I could've blown up the house and killed myself. We did get rid of that oven, and I thank the Lord for sparing my life.

In the next few weeks, Elvis Presley died. The city went a little crazy. I was lying low to let my hair grow back, and after that, I was ready to get out and party. My cousin next door, named James, had recently returned from the army and was acting kind of crazy. His nickname was Frog. He was taking me and my brother to a club, we had a few drinks before we got there and smoked a few joints. He paid our way in the club. We weren't in there for more than five minutes. The next thing I knew, James was kicking somebody's ass, and the guard was breaking it up. He told James to leave, but you know the deal. James wouldn't stop talking or leave fast enough, so they called the police. I tried to tell the police I was new in town and didn't know where we were at. He thought I was trying to be funny and grabbed me. When they grabbed me, my brother grabbed him. The next thing you know, we were all handcuffed and on our way to jail. My brother and I had never been to jail before. All I could think of was I got to be hard. I was not going to be a wimp. When we finally got booked and were put in a cell, people kept saying, "That's where James Earl Ray was being held in the jail." I was pretending as if none of that shit bothered me. But that happened on a Thursday night, and if we didn't get bailed out by a certain time on Friday, we couldn't get out until Monday.

My mother came through as always and got us out just before lockdown. James refused for someone to pay for him. He said that he was going to stay. I guess that he knew since he was a veteran, they were not going to hold him, and the next day he was back home.

We never went to a club with him again. My days in Memphis were up and down from then on. Most of James's friends became our friends. I ended up hanging out with Snake. Since I had a car, most of the time, I would drive people around to do stupid shit, like going to get weed or going to the crap house or going to sell stolen shit. I would drive Snake around to look for cars to break into. Then we would go sell whatever he got. Next, we would go to the crap house, and he would lose all the money. We used to break in the train that ran in our neighborhood. We never knew what was going to be on the trains. We just wanted some money, and we did whatever we needed to do to get it.

I hung out with Snake. He had brothers and sisters that were in and out of jail. So they went for bad. They all gave me my respect, so I was cool with everybody. We had a club right in the middle of our hood called Club Rosewood. Disco hound was the d.j. and the assistant manager's name was Linda. She became my girl the first day that I walked in the club. So she never charged me for anything that I wanted. I could take anybody I wanted with me. At that time, there were still lots of pimps in Memphis, and some of them would come in the club from other parts of Memphis. Once one of those pimps tried to take my girl and some of my boys came and told me, I whupped his ass in the restroom one night, and I didn't get static from nobody. Then I started staying over my girlfriend's house, which was in his hood. I never had another problem with him; however, I never tried to be a gangster either.

One day everything almost came to a screeching halt when Snake came to my house. I was about to drop my brother and a couple of his coworkers off at work. My brother rode with me. Something seemed wrong to me, and I couldn't figure it out. So after I dropped them off, he said, "Let's go get some money." I thought that he wanted to go to the crap house, the one that we had gone to the night before. He had won about $300. However, he wanted to go and rob somebody or to break in a car. I didn't want to do that at the time because I had gas in my car. He had filled my tank up, and I had some money from last night, and I didn't want to rock the boat. We had been doing well; nevertheless, we tried to break in a few cars but couldn't. Then he climbed a fence, and still he didn't find anything. Then he spotted a big truck that was full of tools sitting behind a building. There was only one way in and one way out. I let him out the car so he could go check it out while I turned the car around. That way, we could be headed out. Just as I got turned around, I heard a glass break, and whoever owned the truck had heard the glass break. All I can remember seeing was my friend running toward the car. A guy was chasing him, and he was also hollering, "Call the police!" I pushed the door open while driving slowly enough for him to jump into the car. Then I pulled off, the police was trying to get my license plate number. We had to go all the way back around the building and back to the street, and then we got away. It seemed like it took forever. I could only hear sirens coming. I was zooming through traffic, and all of a sudden, we got to the light, and my car cut off. The sirens were getting louder and louder. We jumped out the car, and we pushed the car off to the side of the road as the police zoomed past us. I don't know why my car cut off, but I do know if it hadn't cut off, they would have caught us, and we would've gone to jail. I started that car up and drove to Rosewood.

I dropped Snake off at the corner and drove home. I pulled out that phone book and called a junkyard and told them to come and get that car. I prayed that the police wouldn't come and knock on my door. That was the end of my hoodlum days.

My girls would go to my mother's house and pick me up. I was cool with that. Linda and I dated for a couple of years. I met another lady at the corner Store, across the street from the club. Terri understood that I was not the typical brother from the streets. She talked me into going back to school. My life really changed. Both ladies were still in my life. Linda was sweet. She would allow me to drive her car. I lived with Linda for two years, but I could never turns our relationship around. Terri helped me to enroll in school. Wow! She was beautiful, sweet and she didn't have any children. Linda, beautiful and sweet as momma's apple pie and had two children. I was like their father. Terri end up being my wife because she talked me into going back to school, and that's what changed my life. I went to LeMoyne-Owen College, and the two things I wanted to do most was play baseball, which I thought was my best talent, and learn photography. My photography bug came from my neighbor, coach, and friend Gene "Bowlegs" Miller. We were hanging out in clubs 2001 and Place Disco. There was a photographer named Pierre. He was a cool brother. All the ladies were trying to get free pictures from him. I thought I could do that.

I was having the time of my life. However, I must admit that I spent more time at a club called the Place Disco. I hope you get the idea. When the entertainment bug first hit me, I didn't know how or when; I just knew that I would be involved in entertainment in one way or the other.

Anyway, the more I would see Pier, the cooler we became. One day I had car trouble, and I was walking over to one of my friend's house. On a hot summer day in Memphis, Tennessee, I was sweating like a pig, cars were zooming past me like mad, when all of a sudden, a car stopped and backed up. I looked to see who was this stopping for me. To my surprise, it was Pier. He had so much junk on his car seats and floors, he had to move things around to make room for me to get into his car. As I was picking up some of the pictures and helping him to put them back in the boxes, I noticed that he had pictures of Michael Jackson on the floor that had been taken from all angles. When I asked him where he had gotten all those pictures from, he told me that he shot them during the Off the Wall Tour. I was so impressed with him, Pier became my inspiration. We kept on driving down the street. And as he stopped so I could get out the car, I asked him if I could have one of the pictures of Michael Jackson, and he said, "Yes, take whatever you want." It really wasn't a big deal to him.

That ride really served me in more ways than I realized it would at that time. When I look back at that moment, I now realize how much that particular, situation define what I really wanted to do with my life. I told myself if I made it doing photography, I would also help someone else and give them a start the same way Pier had done for me.

Within two months, I excitedly enrolled in LeMoyne Owen College with a major in—you guessed right—photography. I kept a camera with me twenty-four hours a day. I got on people's nerves because I was always taking pictures somewhere.

One day I was driving to school, and I heard on the radio that Prince and the Revolution was going to be at the coliseum that night. Now I never liked Prince— until one morning, I was watching the *Today Show* they previewed *Purple Rain*. Now at this time, I never liked Prince—none of his songs moved me much, but *Purple Rain* changed all that. It was a great movie to me. While I was driving, I just turned my car around and headed to the coliseum. It was about noon; the show wasn't going to start until 8:00 p.m., so I parked my car, got my camera out, and walked right in with his stage crew. I walked all over the place. I finally found a newspaper and went to a seat on the side of the stage. I read the paper until somebody came to get there seat. I moved over to another seat. I was in a great seat by the time the show started.

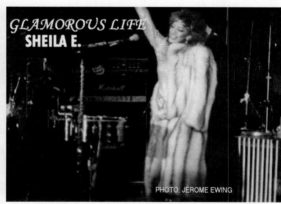

These were the first pictures of stars in my collection, I am very proud of them. Soon after that, I became a very good photographer. My second break was by a secretary at the college. She was involved in a fashion show at a small nightclub. She would see me with my camera all the time, and she asked me if I could go and take some pictures of her. I did not know that a small hole in the wall club would kick open some pretty big doors for me. For two reasons, I was on the LeMoyne-Owen baseball team, and with the level of talent I had, I met ex-musician Gene "Bowlegs" Miller, who had worked with Etta James and Ann Peebles and Maurice White, who started Earth, Wind & Fire. They had gone to school together at Booker T. Washington in Memphis. They also worked with other Chess Record artists. Bowlegs loved coaching, and I was his number one player. If I couldn't get a ride to a game, he would come to get me. We won the city softball championship in 1985. He

was so happy. Bowlegs was a talker, he finally had something to brag about. At that time, Bowlegs was the southeast distributor for Island Records. He would let me meet some of the artists that would come to Memphis. Bowlegs would always give us records. That opportunity really

started my entertainment juices flowing. Remember the small club that I told you about called First Place that I went to on the day of the fashion show? Well, on that same day, I met the owner, Odell Tidwell. His soundman was named Robert McKesson, and he was also the soundman for the Bar-Kays soul group. Sometimes

you have to make a break in order to get a break. So once I found out that they had backstage passes to all the events that came to Memphis, I had to figure out how to go with them. So I told Tidwell to let me go with him backstage and get pictures with all the stars and blow them up and put them on the

wall at the club. He thought that was a great idea, and suddenly we became a three-partner team. From 1983 to 1985, we went to all the shows that came to Memphis. Some of those shows were Kurtis Blow, the Commodores, the Bar-Kays, Mary James Girls, Kool & the Gang, Rev. Jesse Jackson, and many others. In 1983, while still in school, I got a job at a fairly new company called Federal Express. While working there, I took advantage of the opportunity to jump-seat (in airline terms), which meant that a FedEx employee could fly free while sitting in the cockpit with the pilots.

One day while at a carwash, I was showing off some of my pictures, and William Bedford pulled up to wash his car. I had watched Memphis State get beaten in the Sweet 16 Tournament, and Bedford was the center, and he had a pretty good year. I couldn't believe another opportunity just fallen into my lap. However, understanding that things happen for a reason, I adopted that cliché at that time. So I eased my way over there and started talking, and *bam!* I whipped out my pictures and asked him if he had a photographer going to the NBA draft with him.

He replied, "No."

Then I told Him that I worked at Federal Express and that I could jump-seat to New York and be his photographer. When I look back on that day, I get chills because I had to be very stupid at that time. Bedford said, "Okay," and then he gave me his phone number. I believed him; therefore, when I went to work that night, I made reservations with the jump-seat office. Then on the same night that I was to leave, I must have called William Bedford at least twenty-five times. I never did get an answer. I believe that the average person would've said "The hell with that" and cancelled and forgot about it. Not me! I got on the plane with no return jump-seat ticket, with only twenty-eight dollars in my pocket—stupid—without any friends or family in New York. Stupid!

As we approached New York for our landing, I began to pray. I didn't know where I was going and what was about to happen. I could see Yankee Stadium, and the sunrise was so nice, really bright orange. I think I blinked out for a few  minutes because the next thing I member was walking down the plane roll-up stairs. I walked around asking people where the NBA draft was happening. Someone finally told me it was at the Madison Square Garden. I had to ask about seven or eight taxi drivers to take me there. No one wanted to take me. Finally, this one driver said, "Come, I'll take you." He charged me twenty-five dollars for the trip. I only had three dollars left in my pocket. Then it really hit me—I'm in trouble. God was with me all day, as I walked to Waldorf Astorian Hotel, I could see a crowd of people and all the players arriving. I got very excited and yelled, "Bedford! Bedford!"

Bedford looked up and saw me and said, "there my father. You can stay with them."

The first thing I said was, "Thank you, God! Amen!"

Mr. Bedford, his sister and girlfriend.

Bedford's father was a really nice man. His sister and his girlfriend wanted to know who I was and why I was tagging along.

Mr. Bedford said, "Bill told him to stay with us."

My mind wasn't really on those pictures at the moment, but that was what I was there for. *I'll worry about getting home later*, I thought. Now I got a garment bag and a camera bag to carry around with me. I stayed in the lobby, and I got a chance to meet Peal Washington, Roy Tarpley, and Len Bias, along with Kenny "Sky" Walker. By now, I was very hungry and managed to get a free Coke and some cheese and crackers. When it was time for us to go to Madison Square Garden, we all loaded up in a limo. William Bedford rode there in the car with the other basketball players. I felt so good walking around in Madison Square Garden through the crowd.

While there, I saw David Stern and Rick Barry. Everything went so fast; by the time we got inside the draft had started, Len Bias was being called. As I walked up the stage, Len walked right by me. As the ESPN camera was rollin' ten minutes later,

Bedford's name was called, and just that fast, it was time to go. Man, with all that interaction, it felt like a dream to me. Time passed really fast, and we all loaded back up in the limo. Once we got settled in, someone asked the limo driver to take us on a tour. That gave me one

more opportunity to break out the camera. We went to the Statue of Liberty and the Twin Towers and to get something to eat. After the tour, the million-dollar question came up.

We were headed to the airport, and I was asked, "Where can we drop you off?" My life flashed in front of me! Then I started thinking, *Am I going to be a*

41

bum? Stuck on the streets of New York? And I don't know anybody. Next, we rode to a couple of Federal Express Stations to see if they could help me. I was thinking that maybe they could advance a jump-seat-ticket privilege for me. That didn't work either. Then I tried calling home, and all I got was the answering machine. Even if they did answer, I already knew that they didn't have any money. After about an hour facing the need to get to the airport, the crew figured out that I was not going to leave them, Mr. Bedford finally said, "I am going to buy him a ticket." Believe me, this was certainly an unhappy flight home for me. I really think that I grew up as a person that day. Thank you again, Mr. Bedford! The next morning after not sleeping at all, I turned on the TV and saw that Len Bias was found dead. I was in shock. I had just seen him hours ago, and now he was gone, and the highlight on ESPN showed him walking past me. That moment is now part of my history.

After that meltdown, I was in bed one night, and my phone rang at about 2:00 am. Mr. Tidwell was on the line, and he said, "Guess who just walked in to my club?"

I remember thinking, *It better be Pam Grier.*

Then he said, "It is Stevie Wonder."

My reply to him was "Stop lying."

Then he said, "Why would I call you this time of the night with some bullshit. You'd better grab your camera and get your ass down here."

By the time I got there on Beale Street, Stevie Wonder was just getting his food. Then I whipped out my camera and took a shot while he was eating. The next thing I knew, this big-ass man grabbed me, looked me in the eyes, and said, "No pictures while he's eating!" Next, he said that if I did that again, he was going to take my camera.

Then I said to him, "Sorry, I didn't know."

Then he said, "I knew you didn't know. That's why I didn't take your camera."

As we stared at each other, I noticed that there was something about him that I liked. He looked at me and said, "Cool out. You will get a chance to take some pictures."

The nightclub was about to close, and there were only about eight or nine people in the room. I hadn't even noticed that one of the people in the room was my music teacher over at LeMoyne-Owen College. His name was Herman Green. I went over to him and spoke to him, and we talked for a minute. Then Mr. Green told me to hold on for a minute. Next, he grabbed his

saxophone and just started playing. I could tell that he was finished for the night and that he was packing up for the night. Everybody else had already gone home by then. However, I guessed that he was thinking like me, *Damn, let me put on a show!*

While Stevie Wonder was sitting there, he played one or two more songs. By then, Stevie Wonder did something that the eight or nine remaining will never forget or probably ever witness in life again. Stevie got up from his table and went to the piano and gave us a personal concert. I was the only one in the room with

a camera. *Wow*, how lucky can you get! Thank you, Lord.

By that time, I had started building a nice portfolio: the Commodores, Stevie Wonder, the Temptations, and Freddie Jackson from the Blues Awards.

Then I heard that Stevie Wonder was staying at the Peabody Hotel, and I was feeling very lucky, so I went down to the Peabody the next day to see if I could possibly get a few more shots.

44

While taking these shots, I ran into Ollie Woodson of the Temptations in the lobby of the Peabody Hotel. While talking to him, he introduced me to the person who would take me to the next level later in my life.

However, at this time, I didn't know that. Martha and Keith Frye both had a lot of clout in the music business back in the '80s. Keith was southeast director for Capitol Records. Martha was director for MCA Records. They both lived in Atlanta, and they gave me their cards, which I still have today.

In 1986, I just up and decided to move to Atlanta. That brought back memories of the New York trip because I didn't know anyody in Atlanta. I didn't have any family or money, just like in New York, but I went on and put in my request for a transfer. And for some strange reason, I actually got the job. I had a small going-away party at Tidwell's place. I remember praying before I left, because I didn't know what was about to happen. I loaded up my car, bought a map, and took off for Atlanta. I had three hundred dollars in my pocket, and a job was waiting for me that paid thirteen dollars an hour. Little did I know that when I arrived in Atlanta, it would take me a couple of weeks to receive my first paycheck. I was so accustomed to getting my check once a week. Then I found myself back in trouble again. I can truly say that the Lord has always stayed on my side.

The Atlanta Years

In the mid-'80s, while working at Federal Express in Memphis, Tennessee, I decided to move to Atlanta, Georgia. It was spring 1986 after a great going-away party at Tidwell's club, with my car packed to the rim, that I left Memphis, Tennessee, at 3:00 a.m., and I got to Atlanta about nine or ten in the morning. In those days, there was no GPS. I had a map, and I still had to stop to get directions, but I finally made it to College Park, Georgia. That was where the FedEx ramp was, so I got a room nearby for $49.99 a night if booked for two nights. Little did I know those would be my best two nights for a while. I went to the FedEx ramp to meet my manager and coworkers. Both of them were from Memphis. In fact, Reginald Cofield was a star basketball player from Southside High School, which was right across the street from where we moved to in Memphis. We became good friends. So now I was feeling a lot better. All I needed now was to get my paycheck, which was being sent overnight by FedEx. Three days went by, still no check. My money was almost gone. I didn't have money for my room, and my car was packed with my clothes and a big-ass thirty-five-inch TV that took up the whole backseat. Reginald had told me about the trailer park where you could rent a room for $120 a week, but I didn't have that much left, so I had to sleep in my car. Now it was starting to get tough. There were other people in the same boat as me, and most of them went back home. I was not going to give up. The Lord hadn't ever let me down before. I felt he brought me here for some reason, so after praying, I needed some place to park. I remembered for lunch we would go to a place called Draf House, which today is called Chick Fila. They stayed open twenty-four hours a day, and they were around the corner from the ramp. My manager told me he had found out that my check would come on Friday, and it was Tuesday. I thought, what could I do to make it a few more days? There were showers for the trucker drivers, I used them. That was helpful. As I got back to my car and turned the radio on, I heard, "Come to Mr. V's tonight." Dominique Wilkins and the Atlanta Hawks were going to be there, and Hakeem "the Dream" Olajuwon of the Houston Rockets was special guest. I don't know why that meant anything to me at this time, but it was heaven-sent. I was just trying to survive, but something kept telling to go to Mr. V's tonight. So with my uniform still on, I took off for Mr. V's. I didn't have much gas and just had about eleven or twelve dollars in my pocket. As I got there, I said another prayer. My thinking was, *There must be some rich women in there. Let's see what I can do.* I got to the door, and the girl taking money had just stepped away for a minute, so I walked in. I said, "Thank you, Lord," because that saved me ten dollars.

As I got in, all the ballplayers were there, so I was walking around thinking, *Why am I here?* I noticed a table of good-looking women. They were looking at me. Now that would have been great any other time, but not tonight. I learned not to go asking women anything if you don't have any money, because one of them will say yes. So I was there about thirty minutes, and there wasn't anything happening for me, so I thought, *Go get a beer and get the hell out of here with seven or eight dollars.* As I was walking to the bar, I saw somebody I knew. I didn't know his name, but he was on the LeMoyne-Owen College basketball team. Man! I walked up to him, and we started talking. He remembered me; I was on the baseball team. His name was Sam Townsend; he was there with his boys. He was in the same situation I was in; he was sleeping on the couch over somebody's house. He told me he had put in for his own apartment. It was going to be about two weeks before it was ready. I asked him, "Could I share it with you? I'll pay half of everything."

He said, "Cool."

We both worked at FedEx but at different stations. I was cool now. I got out of there as fast as I could, feeling like my God was awesome. I still had to make it two more weeks. "How can you do that?" a coworker asked me. The Lord brought me this far; he wouldn't let me down. The first week was tough; my back started hurting that Saturday when I got off work. I got in my car and rode downtown for no reason at all, parked my car on the street, and started walking. When I got to Peachtree Street, I could see a crowd of people following somebody. As I got closer, I saw it was Muhammad Ali. I thought about going back to the car to get my camera, but by the time I would have gotten back he would have been gone. I followed everybody until he made it to the hotel. As everybody was walking away, I noticed this girl looking at me. She asked for my name. I asked for hers. We struck up a good conversation.

She said, "Let's go get something to eat." She was buying.

That was music to my ears, so I said, "Okay."

While eating, I told her what was happening with me. She was from Seattle, Washington, visiting by herself, and didn't know anybody. I thought, *Wow!*

She said I could stay in her room for the two days she had left. I was thinking, *Is this real?* She made it clear she did not want to have sex. I thought, *Cool. Having a bed was good enough for me.*

One morning as she was packing and I was leaving for work, she gave me $200 and told me to get a room; because she didn't want me sleeping in my car. I stood there in shock. "I just met you. Why are you being so nice?" I asked.

She said, "You are a nice guy, and that's what I want to do."

Just like that, we exchanged numbers, and I left. Her name was Vicky, I would see her again. Speeding to get to work I got stopped by the police, but for some reason, he didn't give me a ticket. I was thinking I got favors with God. I thank my Lord for everything he has done in my life. I didn't take anything for granted. I could pay for the room until Friday and wait for Sam to call and let me know the apartment was ready. I didn't hear from Sam until Saturday morning; he told me they said it was going to be another week. I had tears in my eyes; I was ready to give up. *How can I make it another week?* But my Lord was not going to let me down.

Monday, my check came, and it was four weeks' pay. I thanked the Lord about a hundred times. Now all I had to do was cash my check and wait for Friday. Well the bank said I had to deposit and wait a couple of days. Sam called to tell me what the deposit was, we couldn't move in until Saturday. I only had $100 left, but

I didn't care. I remember when I finally move all that stuff out of my car into my own apartment. I said "Thank you Lord" numerals of times. I felt really blessed. If any one of those things hadn't happened, I would have been headed back to Memphis in bad shape, but instead, I was about to go on a magical journey that only the Lord could have laid out.

Okay now, here was the situation: I was single, had my own apartment, a Good job at FEDEX, I was living in the hottest city in the world. And I was happy. I weathered a big storm, and now I can laugh again. Sam and I would split the rent and light bill, because I got money. I never had a roommate, that was going to be different, but Sam and I, we were glad to have each other. Sam was a workaholic, and I wasn't; he didn't like to go out to clubs, and I did; we were living in Dunwoody, Georgia, which, at the time, was one of the most expensive places to live. We were two different people; he was working days and overtime, and I was working night and didn't want overtime. So we were never there at the same time until Sundays for the first year,

then I became a courier. He was working in Marietta, Georgia, and I was in Norcross, Georgia. I had to go to courier school; it was held at our district office, and I remember one day I thought I would never make it. What happened was, I was in school at the time. Classes were held at our district office. There was about fifteen to twenty people in our class. Only four or five of us were smokers, and our teacher let us know that the only place where we could smoke was in his office. His office was on the fourth floor, and that was cool with us. So every day on break, we would go to his office and smoke. It was no big deal.

Then one day while on break, I went to the restroom and then to his office. Nobody was there. So I sat at his desk, reclined back, and I was enjoying my smoke. All of a sudden, the door opened, and in walked Fred Smith, FedEx's

CEO. There I was, all kicked back. My heart stopped for a minute. He walked in and shook my hand and walked out. Some big wheel was with him. I remember thinking, *This is it. I am fired.* Well, about a month later, the policy changed. No more smoking was allowed in FedEx's buildings. I was sorry that I was the one who got caught. I believe that it was going to happen at some point. Then I was called in to work overtime, something I'd never done. I finally said yes, so I went into get my packages. Halfway through my route, I noticed a package going to MCA Records. I thought, *I'm going to deliver that package last,* at the end of my route, I walked into MCA Records and asked for Janice Burley, which was the name on the package I got to sign for, then I asked her who was in charge of hiring photographers. She let me know it was her. I told her I had taken pictures of the Bar-Kays, Stevie Wonder, Prince, And others. I would like to take pictures of any artists you have coming in town. She told me to bring my pictures the next time I was out that way. Well, guess what, as soon as I got off work, I went back. She looked at my pictures and liked them, then she told me who the artists were that she had coming. I told her I could do all of them. Little did I know what I thought was a big break for me was about to get even bigger. I think Janice was working on the Polygram Records side, which was with MCA Records, but MCA bought Motown, and they moved to a big new building, and it was on my route, so now I could go there every day. Remember, when I was in Memphis, I met a lady from

BOBBY WOMACK

Atlanta who was the southeast director for MCA Records. That lady was Marth Frye Thomas. She was now over both branches with the merge, and now the list of stars was huge. Bobby Brown had left New Edition and signed with MCA, so did Guy, Heavy D & the Boyz, Patti LaBelle, Elton John, Bobby Womack, Boyz II Men, Smokey Robinson, Stevie Wonder, I felt everything I had gone through was now paying off.

Bobby Brown   Johnny Gill

Jerome Ewing
Original

welcome to laface records
PHOTO: JEROME EWING

SUPERSTARS OF SPORTS

I was assigned to shoot Smokey Robinson at a downtown Atlanta Hotel, one of Smokey's last release parties where all the dignitaries in Atlanta were there. It was just a wonderful evening. As the party was coming to an end and I was packing up my gear and looking for a restroom, I saw a big brother walking down the hallway. It seemed like he was looking for the restroom also. He looked like an athlete—he looked like Hershel Walker; he went in the restroom, then I went in. It was him. While taking care of my business, I was thinking, *Should I ask for an autograph?* Better yet, I was wondering if I should take a picture or what. After he left the restroom, I slowly went behind him. I then noticed a checkpoint up ahead, so I caught up with him and started talking, as we walked pass the checked point, we walk inside this big-ass ballroom and every sport legend from every major sport was there: Dan Marino, Sugar Ray Leonard, and Wayne Greziky, the hockey player. I would walk around among all those sports stars and try to shake hands with as many of them as I possibly could. I was thinking to myself, if I would pull my camera out, someone would ask me whom I was shooting for. And I would have to have the right answer, so I couldn't hesitate with the right answer, or they would kick me out. So I waited awhile and just enjoyed myself. When the party started to wane, I whipped my camera out and got as many shots as I could. Some of them were cool with it. That was my second time meeting Muhammad Ali, I have also met-Thomas Hearns, Roy Jones Jr., and Joe Frazier and Atlanta stars Mick Luckherst, Gaylord Perry, David Justice, Dominick Wilkins, Dionne Sanders, and Evander Holyfield.

I was happy to be there when Mayor Bill Campbell gave Jermaine Dupree the key to the city of Atlanta.

M. C. Hammer was a big thrill for me for a couple of reasons. First of all, I didn't know everybody knew Hammer. He was a batboy for Oakland A's baseball team, and I was a Reggie Jackson fan. I loved those Charlie Finley–era uniforms! Baseball used to be my life. Secondly, Charlie Finley gave Hammer the money to get started. He sold his records out of the trunk of his car, and that was something that I was also doing at that time (street hustling). Thirdly, it was ironic that he was a dancing fool and that he carried lots of dancers with him. At that time, I also was a dancing fool. Therefore, when I found out that he was going to the club, that I call my house, it was a night to be remembered. It seemed as if dances were breaking off all over the club. Hammer and Tone Loc cut up all night long.

I was balancing partying and capturing memorable moments. Besides being very gracious, M. C. Hammer was very cool. Nonetheless, the party was very fierce that particular night. Hammer spent more time with the crowd, than on the stage. What was special about that era is that people did not have access to cameras like they do in this day and time. There were no such things as cell phones, iPhones, or iPads. Most people had disposable cameras only if they were throwing a party or having a party of their own. Club Sensation was the

place to be at that time. They would bring acts in the city like Guy, Tony! Toni! Toné! Bobby Brown, Johnny Gill, Peabo Bryson, Rob Base, Al B. Sure! After 7, and many, many more. I had an unlimited access to all these famous people. It is something about being in the right place at the right time. I will cover more about some of these photos in the following chapters.

"Stevie Wonder, Happy Birthday"—I can't hear that song without seeing Stevie onstage with Peabo Bryson, Jean Carnes, and Al B. Sure! This was the first official Martin Luther King holiday, this was a day to be proud and it was an honor to be part of it. Dexter King was representing the King family. I also met and started a friendship with Altovise Davis (Sammy Davis Jr.'s wife).

In my opinion, Altovise Davis did not get enough credit for having a big part for making this historic day possible. (Dr. Martin Luther King a National Holiday). Thought I would see Dexter King more after that historic day. That day will always be special to me. I was sad when Altovise Davis died. Bobby Womack and I lost contact with her. Hope someone would pay tribute to her someday.

Al B. Sure! I once took a picture of Al B. Sure! backstage, and it took better than the 8 × 10 Pro he was using, so I was hired to take pictures at a live show. I'm still thinking about how I was able to capture so many moments of the stage life back then! Al wasn't as personable as some of the other artists were, but I was still able to spend lots of time around him. One of the special things he did was that he helped some of the other artists become even bigger than he was. Peabo Bryson and I have lots of definitive views of Peabo. I was once his FedEx deliveryman. I had delivered packages to his condo and once played basketball with him. (Keep singing.) However, I was glad to see Peabo go to Community City with those wild-ass players, sign up like everybody else, and play ball. He got beat real bad, Bam! I laughed my ass off. Peabo's got guts, but he was not a great basketball player, but he was a singing M-F. Speaking of basketball, let me throw this out there.

While I was working at FedEx, I had knee surgery, and my rehab was with the Atlanta Hawks and GT player Mark Price at sport. Mark Price was with Cleveland and Remel Robinson Hawk, ex-76er Andrew Toney, and Craig Ehlo. I can say I hold my own. When I saw Jordan hit that shot on Ehlo, I felt bad for him. Andrew Toney was still a shooting M-F. I wish I could capture those days and put them in a bottle. (Sidebar: there are two more sports moments on a national level that I think about because they are shown all the time—the 1986 Draft, the death of Len Bias. I had stood where Len walked in front of ESPN cameras.) Michael

Jordan was hitting that shot on Craig Ehlo after being in rehab with Ehlo. There were other ballers—Tyne Hill, William Bedford, Peal Washington, Kenny "Sky" Walker, Cliff Livingston, John Battle, Doe Rivers, Ray Allen, and Elliott Perry.

My daughter was visiting me in Atlanta, and I took her to MCA Records to meet Martha Fry Thomas. I parked my car and got out. As I was walking toward the building, out came this skinny lady—sorry to say—who looked a little out of it. Her hair wasn't tight, something I was used to seeing from black women. She had on white boots. It was Mary J. Blige, and she looked at me and said, "Damn, don't go anywhere. We will be back."

My daughter burst out laughing!

Martha said, "This is a new artist, named Mary J. Blige."

Well, to be honest, since so many artists were coming and going so fast, only one out of ten would make it. I actually thought Mary J. Blige wasn't going to make it.

A month later, my daughter called me, all excited, saying, "Dad, turn on *In Living Color.*"

I jumped up and turned to *In Living Color*, and there she was, Mary J. Blige, stepping out with a long *Cat in the Hat* look, doing her thing. I was in shock; I learned a lesson that I will never forget. Never judge a book by its cover. I did wait about thirty minutes before we left. Sometimes I wonder what would have happened if I just waited, to talk to the Cat in the Hat, as I now think of Mary J. Blige.

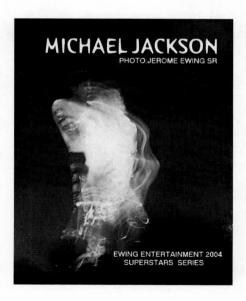

THE MICHAEL JACKSON HOOKUP

One day I hoped to go in-depth about some of the pictures and stories in this book. Some of these stories brought on many of my blessing. Here is a sample of what I'm talking about. If you read early in my book, while I was living in Memphis, Tennessee, a friend called me at 2:00 a.m. to tell me that Stevie wonder just walked into his club, he wanted me to come down and bring my camera. I walked in and saw Stevie Wonder sitting at a table eating I walk up and started taking pictures.

At that point, one of his guys who worked as Stevie's bodyguards grabbed me and was talking about taking my camera, but he chilled, and all was cool. Fast Forward to 1988 or 1989, when Michael Jackson was at the Omni I had a backstage pass, Oh yes! I had swag about myself. I could get into any show. After walking into checkpoints, I was cool. I would walk back out so I could smoke, on my way back in, I saw two boys they were around twelve or thirteen years of age. They begged me to help them to get in because they loved Michael Jackson. You know being a kindhearted person, so I did help them to get in. They gave me a high five like brothers do, then they went their way, and I went mine. When I got to the checkpoint to get back in, I reached for my pass, and it was gone. I was so hurt because I felt like a fool. I helped somebody, and they got me. That was dumb of me, but God had my back. Because out of nowhere came the guy, that was Stevie Wonder's bodyguard. He looked at me and said something. Then I said, "Are you Stevie Wonder's bodyguard, do you remember me?"

Then he said something like "Yeah, I remember you."

Then we struck up a conversation, and I started walking with him like we were buddies. That is pretty much the key to getting into functions. You should just act like you are supposed to be there. I

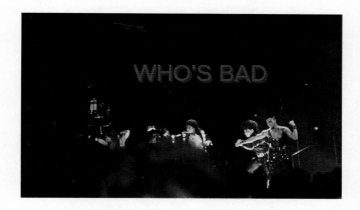

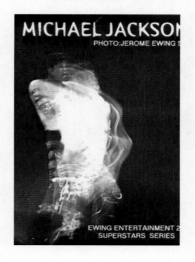

didn't care what they say. You must act like you supposed to be there. I was about 150 feet of Michael Jackson, I still didn't have a pass, I had to keep my camera hidden. I did managed to take a few pictures before I left. I was on my way home from work. That was the coolest pit stop I ever made. I would always do stuff like that just to see if I could get in. There were a lot of things going on with me at that time.

I was working at Federal Express in the daytime, and I was up all night with my entertainment business. I also had my girl from Memphis living with me. There was very little time for sleep in my life. I was on a twenty-four-hour spin cycle. I was living at a pace that was doomed to explode at some point. There was so much happening I didn't have time to think about it. I wanted it all, and I paid the price, especially with my family and son. Instead of being on the baseball field with Dave Justice, Dionne Sanders, helping with homework, watching a movie with my family. Instead, I was hanging out with the movie stars. If I could touch one person life, keeping them from making the same mistake, writing this book was not in vain. When I compiled a lists of celebrities I have in my collection, I get goose bumps.

Some of those things happened back-to-back, I didn't remember some until I saw the pictures. Lisa McCall from Motown said, "Jerome always finds a way to get in one of the pictures."

"Oops." I lost a lot of pictures in a flood in 1995 in Atlanta, such as Muhammad Ali, Johnnie Taylor, and many more. This book is not intended to talk about how great I am. Instead, it is to let you know how blessed you can be if you allow the Lord to direct your future. Your destiny is your destiny, one that only you can complete. When it's all said and done, you can miss God's destiny for your life, "Your choice". You might find out what happening in your life it's just a chapter in your story, not the final act. There are greater things ahead. You never know how many lives you can affect in a positive way if you keep a positive attitude. Well, that's how I feel. I believe that there is more to come for me in my life.

KID 'N PLAY AND MARTIN AND JEROME

Oh, how about this, MCA Records hired me to shoot pictures for the Jack the Rapper Convention. They were promoting the soundtrack for *House Party 2* or *3*. The Pajama Jam and Kid 'n Play were going to perform. So the MCA seats began filling up fast. I was there two hours early to help with the setup. There were women everywhere. You couldn't take five steps without seeing fine women (it was five women to one man, as we used to say). I had a handful of women some of them were trying to see the show and receive the giveaway. I remember taking pictures with some of the ladies, when Kid' N Play arrived. They had Martin Lawrence with them. I may have been looking like a playboy or a player, but I was there to take their pictures for that event. As I look back on that time, I might have been a little cocky, but I was very humble. Kid 'n Play got up and did their thing, and it felt like history was being made, because their first movie was a big hit. It was a good movie, and Martin didn't do a lot of talking. They called him to the stage, he talked about some funny shit, then he left the stage, then around the room. Meanwhile, the girls that I helped to get in to the show were smiling and rubbing up against me. I really made their day, that was really cool with me. Jerome's name was being called all around the room. The girls were calling, "Jerome," MCA staff were calling, "Jerome," and people in the room who wanted whatever pictures were also calling, "Jerome." I was taking care of them. Jerome was the name of the night. I took lots of Vanessa del Rio, a porn star, I was told. So when Martin Lawrence got his own show and I saw the chart, "Jerome," And I saw the outfit he was wearing, I started shaking my head.

You can make up your own mind, but I believe that I am "Jerome" from the *Martin* show. I didn't want any money, I just liked to know. Since I didn't load my photos up on the Internet, people forgot about them after about ten or twenty years. The stories behind the pictures. At that time in my life, I was really being blessed! Every day I didn't understand it, but it was like a wonderful dream. Everything that could go right went right. I was getting calls to photograph so many special people at some important event every day. I can't even remember some of them.

KIM
Burse

I do remember Kim Burse and I making videos of Dionne Farris of *Arrested Development* fame. This opportunity led her to getting the A & R Director at Sony Records. She signed or was part of them signing Beyoncé and Destiny's Child. Kim and I

always worked together on something. Lisa McCall came on the scene and into my life at this time. Lisa has always been a person who didn't want her pictures taken. It was rare to see Lisa on one of my pictures, but she made so much happen for me over a period of time. She had become Jheryl Busby's

JHERYL BUSBY WITH JERMAINE DUPRI

PHOTO:JEROME EWING

right hand at one time. Jheryl Busby had taken over Motown after Barry Gordy. My Motown, MCA, hookup was strong, which led to my BMG, which was Arista Records which started LA Face Records. This led to So So Def Records. This gave me superpower. I could get jobs from Mercury Records, Rap A Lot, Capitol Records, and many more. Then they started popping up everywhere and, ultimately, ran me out of business because the pay dropped pretty quickly. However, the memories are priceless!

I was in photo heaven! Can you believe how I became a major player in the Atlanta music business?

WHAT'S NEXT FOR ME?

Bam! Before I knew what had hits me, I decided that I wanted my own TV show. That thought came from something that happened to me in the '90s. I was all into TV shows, I would get magazines about video-editing technicians, and I would read that in the future, TV would have hundreds of channels. Now, at that time, we had forty to fifty channels, like ESPN, TBS, WGN, HBO, Showtime, local channels, BET, MTV, and a few others. The article I was reading said, there would be new channels and the new channels need programming. I could pick up my video camera and start taping. I thought to myself, I could do that. I would get together with my friend Michael Driftwood and start our own company. Together, we created a video called "Daddy" using a song by Dallas Austin's new group called Highland Place Mobsters. I knew him because Lisa McCall from Motown Records had already asked me to shoot pictures for the wedding of Dallas's sister. Dallas was hot. He had produced hit

songs for Boyz II Men, TLC, and MC McBrain, among others. So by the time Highland Place Mobsters hit the scene, there were so many groups coming to Atlanta. Dallas didn't have time to promote Highland Place Mobsters even though he was in the group. So we saw a reason to make the "Daddy" videos, and it was the only song on the album that I liked. I was trying to get his record company to give me a budget to make videos for the album. It didn't go well, the group broke up. Dallas went back to writing and promoting and ended up discovering Monica and did very well for himself.

Driftwood and I kept on trying. We made a video for the fifth Ward Boyz, and while we were taping that video, Chuck D of Public Enemy walked right into our video. It turned out to be very nice, but in those days, there wasn't any high definition. There was only S-VHS, and the quality was not good enough for BET, and after we tried a few times, we simply gave up. I learned quite a bit from this experience. I learned how to put a video together, edit, shooting angle, and casting. Now, I had met people who wanted videos that didn't necessarily require broadcast quality.

During this period, one of the people I met, whose name is Nicole Rubinstein, had experience in playwriting, and I had opened a photography and video studio in College Park, Georgia. One day I saw this young lady walking through a small strip mall, going door-to-door. She was handing out something, so I invited her in to see what she was handing out. To my surprise, she was selling a little booklet that she had written herself. I got one of the two of them and read it. She had

rewritten *The Wizard of Oz* and *Snow White*. I was impressed, so I asked her if she was interested in turning them into a video. She thought that that was a really great idea, so we set up a casting call, and we ended up with a great cast and taped *The Wizard of Oz* as an interactive video. However, we never had a chance to finish shooting. Nevertheless, I had shot a video with full costumes and a real cast. I wished we had more time to finish it, but it did help both of us. I never heard from her again. I bet she still writing great stories. I hope I get another chance to see her.

From that perspective, I had my new business partner, whom I will call the Boss, whose real name is Tina Remy or Marilyn Shotwell. We invested a lot of money in

a movie called *Space Kid*. The movie was targeted for Nickelodeon. We hired a director. I was the soundman and light man. We held a talent search. Both of us invested a lot of time and money into this project. Every detail was handled in professional manner, but something went wrong. We lost lots of money in trying to make a movie. I wanted to take charge of this project, but the Boss said no, and she had invested most of the money. Therefore, I backed off. I know that I could've made five movies off the money we spent. At that time, it was too expensive to buy equipment, so we rented everything and hired a director. We learned a lot. I felt bad. I told myself *I* could make my own movies.

Nevertheless, I was blessed to be in a big-budget movie. When I was working for FedEx every day, I would deliver a package to an office in downtown Atlanta. There was no name on this office door, and there was an old white man who worked there. He had a beard like that of Wolfman Jack, and his name was Lou. We would talk, and he was just a cool person. One day while I was delivering his package, he was not there. Then in about two to three days, I asked, what had happened to Lou?

The lady that was taking his place said, "Do you know who Lou is?"

And I said, "No, all I know is that he is a Cool dude."

Then she said, "His name is Lou Scroller."

Again I said, "Okay, who is he?"

Then she said, "Have you ever seen the movie called *Scarface*?"

I said, "Yeah, it's one of my favorite movies."

"How about *Sea of Love*?" she said.

"Yes, I've seen that one too," I said.

Then she said that Lou Scroller was the executive producer.

I said, "What!"

She said, "And that's that on that. I probably never see him again. He was there to set up an office, and they were getting ready to start shooting a movie here that's called *The Real McCoy*."

I said, "Damn."

"He didn't say anything about it. That's Lou," she said.

For the next few weeks, more and more people were in the office. By the time they started shooting the movie, it was a full-blown production company. One day I left a box that was a set of Howlin Wolf CDs. I had gotten the box from MCA Records. The next week, I got a letter from Lou asking me if I wanted a part in the movie. Hell, I was thinking not only did I want a part, but I got my wife a part in the movie. I was on cloud nine, as I said in an early chapter, a funny thing happened on the way to the forum. The part Lou gave me was that of a police officer, at the end of the movie, all I had to say but one line. The movie starred Kim Basinger and Val Kilmer. It was about a bank robbery, at the end of the movie as they attempted to make their getaway on the airplane, I stopped the airplane to put some blood organ on it. They thought I was coming after them. My wife played the part of a flight attendant. The movie was filmed at the Atlanta Airport.

The day of the shooting, everything went wrong. We arrived at the airport late. We had no idea, the location in the airport they were shooting. "My God, what else could go wrong?" They made up a name so nobody knew what was going on. By the time we located where they were filming, our parts in the movie were giving to someone else. Director told us that we could be an extra or go back home. We decided to be extras in the movie, that would be better than nothing. As we were walking back and forth like everybody, all I could hear was "*Cut!*" loud and clear. The director walked up to me and said, "Who are you?"

Then I said, "What do you mean?"

Then he said, "Lou wants you to walk up and hold your arms out, and he wants your wife to come up and hug you, Kim Basinger and Val Kilmer will walk in front of you, that's how we are going to shoot this scene."

Damn, I was blown away! Lou stopped his million-dollar production to put me in it.

Someone said, "just because you are in the scene doesn't mean you want be in the final cut."

When the movie came to town I was on the front row, I was in the movie. I said, "Thank you, Lou!"

By now I really have the movie bug. Now it was time to start my own show. I

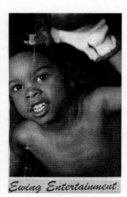

Ewing Entertainment

started a show called *Cool School*. I only made a few episodes in Atlanta, because I moved back to Memphis where I continue my show. Name of the show were change from *Cool School*, to Discovered Memphis. Our first show air in Memphis January 2001. I was blessed to have famous guest appearance on my show both in Atlanta and in Memphis, just to name a few like Denzel Washington, Wesley Snipes, Isaac Hayes, Morgan Freeman, Harry Belafonte, Danny Glover, Sheryl Underwood, Keke Wyatt, Bob Johnson-BET, Avant, Marvin Sease, B. G from Cash Money, among others. I covered the show during the Mike Tyson fight. I also covered the underground railroad during black history month, birthday party shows, and holiday shows. For five years, I funded discovered Memphis without a budget. I had a hardworking, dedicated staff that worked for little or no money. My staff are all doing well now. Sheba Potts-Wright had a hit song that still plays today. It's called "Slow Rollin'," it's a sexy blues tune. Candice been in many commercials, including Campbell's Clinic, Que, tried his hand in Comedy. Derick has his own video production company called DTV with many of today's rap artists. After five years of TV programs, I started a radio show with NBA Memphis State legend William Bedford. We talked about sports, and played Motown old-school music. Let me leave you with this, "All my blessing." I know come from the Lord. I didn't always get paid for everything. I didn't make a lot of money. But I donated an invested back into the community. The Lord has been good to me. The memories I have, the photos, different people that cross my path, artists and the fellowship have been priceless. I wrote my vision and I made it plain, the lord going to bless me with a budget to make my own movie.

My hope in writing this book is to inspire some body, a friend, family, a neighbor, a classmate, how we can move foward with prayer, to be a blessing to someone in our community in a positive way. Everything can't always be about money. Become a leader, encourage someone to stay in school, come up with new ideal, never stop praying. There will be new technology coming up in the near future, that's unbelievable. One thing that will never change is the power of god and the wonderful things he has in store for our future. But we must have love, one for another.

Martin Luther King Jr.

History

When I first found out that I would be moving to Memphis, Tennessee, in 1977, I thought, why? Why Memphis, why now? Well, it didn't take long before God answered that question. First, my first month in Memphis, I was arrested. I was locked up in the same jailhouse that James Earl Ray was locked up in. I thought about jailhouse rock and Elvis. That same month, Elvis Presley died. That was strange.

I stopped by a little company in the curve on a small street in South Memphis. It was a company called Jones Roofing Company. I helped an old man once to build a church. I was a carpenter before moving to Memphis, and we had put the roof on the church ourselves. I needed a job when I arrived in Memphis. I tried this roofing company. They did commercial roofing such as hot tar roofing. I've never done that before. But, Mr. Jones hired me anyway. That was my first job in Memphis, and he started me off with twelve dollars per hour. In 1977, that what they called a good job, and good money. We were putting a roof on the fire station that was positioned right across from the Lorraine Motel. This was done on the tenth anniversary of the assassination of Dr. Martin Luther King Jr. I remember reading about how the FBI had pulled the only black officer off the roof just minutes before the shooting. Now here I am, standing there, scoping the whole view myself. Years later, I left Memphis and moved to Atlanta for no reason at all. I didn't know anybody that lived in Atlanta, and I still ended up putting acts on the stage for the King Fest, and I also ended up meeting the whole King family when they made Dr. Martin Luther King birthday a National Holiday. They sent me a thank-you letter for bringing my artist on the show.

DEXTER KING   JEROME EWING

DEXTER KING
PHOTO JEROME EWING

I moved back to Memphis and ran into Jesse Jackson for the

third time in history. I first saw Jesse Jackson when I was a little boy. I was playing baseball. Somebody hit a baseball over my head, I didn't catch it. The ball rolled across the street, Jesse Jackson picked up the ball and threw it back to me. He was at a place called WSO (West Side Organization). My next-door neighbor was one of the leaders, and Jesse was on the news all the time. That was around 1967 or 1968. Then again in 1981 or 1982, when Jesse Jackson was running for the president of the United States. He stopped in Memphis went backstage to a Kurtis Blow concert Show. I was taking pictures and got a few shots. In 2013, I caught up with him at the Civil Right Museum in Memphis. I had a chance to ask him about the WSO. Then he shook my hand. To sum it up, I was in the same jail that James Earl Ray was in. I was on the fire station rooftop where I had a wide view of the Lorraine Hotel. Where Dr. Martin Luther King assassination occurred.

I was with the man that was on the balcony with Martin Luther King Jr. I was with his wife, son, and daughter.

I don't know what that meant, but it meant a lot to me, Thank you father.

TELL IT LIKE IT WAS

Things can happen so fast it takes years for them to catch up to you! You can live so fast it takes years to understand what accomplishments you have really made. People don't give themselves all the credit that they deserve. We need to evaluate what things are a waste of your time and the things that cost too much to benefit from.

I had to make a painful decision, which was to leave Atlanta so that I could start writing my book. Memphis was my only choice because Memphis is where it all started for me, and my family still lives in Memphis. My incredible experiences include the following:

Prince—1982 Purple Rain Tour

Michael Jackson—1988 Bad Tour

Luther Vandross

PHOTO:JEROME EWING

Stevie Wonder, Al B. Sure!, Jean Carnes
New Edition

Outkast And Heads Of State

EWING ENTERTAINMENT STUDIO

WHITNEY HOUSTON
BUDFEST TOUR EARLY 90'S

Bobby Brown and Whitney Houston

Bobby moved to Atlanta to work on his solo album, I would see him around town. He was the hottest artist in the country, he would still come around when he was in town. MCA Records had hired me to take pictures for Ralph Trezsvant's release party for his solo album, he was on the Budweiser Tour

with Keith Sweat, Babyface, Pebbles, and Whitney Houston.

So after the photo shoot, I managed to get a backstage pass for the show. I had just gotten married, so this show was right on time. The night before the budfest show, I got out and hung around with the crew for a while, now I was married, so I left early. At the show the next day everything was going along smoothly, it was a long break before Whitney came out. She was the headliner; she sang her ass off, then before she left the stage, she said, "I want to introduce to the world my new boyfriend."

Everybody paused for a minute, then Bobby Brown came dancing across the floor. My wife looked at me; we were in shock. Things started to change. Bobby was not hanging out anymore.

I might have been part of the crew Whitney was talking about when she wanted him to stop hanging and spend more time with her, so Bobby moved from Atlanta for a while. Her timing might not have been right for Bobby at that time, because he was red-hot. Bobby Brown is a good guy; he stayed married a long time. When Whitney died, Bobby was here in Memphis getting ready for a show. I ran into him and told him my prayers were with him and wished him all the best.

E. E. FUNNY STORIES

Peabo Bryson—I laugh when I think of Peabo. He probably doesn't want to remember playing basketball with me at the community center. When Peabo

walked by, most of the younger cats didn't know who he was at the time. I was working in MCA Records mailroom. So I knew the guy who was the head of Capitol Records, which was Peabo's record label. I knew Peabo when he went in. I was on the court, and my team lost. After one or two games, Peabo's team played. I knew that this was going to be good, because in warm-up, Peabo was in a different mode from everybody else. We were on speed, and he was on autopilot. You could see how stiff he was, like he hadn't played in years, as their game started. Every time he got the ball, he would call foul; after two or three times, they moved out of his way. As he tried to make a layup, some big-ass dude came out of nowhere and knocked his shot up in the rafters—Bam! Man, we fell out laughing. Everybody in the gym was on the floor. After the game, Peabo walked out of the gym like he had a triple-double. Wish I could have recorded that.

A WILD RIDE

I was driving from downtown Atlanta a couple of days after the Olympics in Atlanta, and I almost got hit by all these cars speeding by me. I was in my FedEx truck. So I followed them as I was on lunch break. I didn't have anything to do. I had my lunch with me, so I went to find out who they were following. I found out that they were following Richard Jewel, who was accused of being the Olympic bomber. I stood outside this house and took pictures on a free camera that FedEx was giving away. The pictures came out like garbage, but being stuck in the moment, he was later cleared of all charges.

MR. FEDEX MAN

Peabo Bryson was on my route in downtown Atlanta. Gaylord Perry—I delivered packages to his house. All the Atlanta Falcons—I delivered packages to their camp. I delivered to the coach of the Denver Broncos Super Bowl Rings, Jimmy Carter library, TNT studio when it was just a little place, I used to meet all the wrestlers. Stolfhers Pine Island is where you can meet the ladies golfers. Paramount Pictures—they would give me movie passes from time to time.

THE PEOPLE MAKERS

These are the people behind-the-scene that makes things happen. Their

talents will never be appreciated. These people live that life. People like Lisa McCall, Karen Tann, Curtis Lord; Bill Williams; Lester Pace; Marie Sellers, the godmother of that era in black music in America; Martha and Keith Frye; Kim Burse; Candice Bonner; Efaye Green; Tony Scott; Earleen Brown; Ed Rucker; and Janice Burley, the lady who gave me my first break.

KIM
Burse

There were so many people that I met on my journey that I can't name them all. Nevertheless, I do remember everybody I ever worked with over the past thirty years. Janet Burley was the most important person on my journey, because if she hadn't believed in me, other things in my life may not have happened. It's all about being the person at the right place at the right time. The thing about me is that I recognize that it is a blessing and a curse. I don't want to be a star or the center of attention. That's just the way I am. I have been on so many big stages, but I have never tried to draw attention to myself, and I really do care about people. You really do hope that people can enjoy a 2014 lifestyle instead of a pre-1900 experience.

WHAT AN HONOR

These are the people I was honored to work with and work for:

Gene "Bowlegs" Miller—Island Records
Odell Tidwell—club owner
Robert "Car Tire" McKesson-Bar-Kay's stage manager
Lou Stroller- Movie Producer
Lisa McCall—Motown-MCA
Karen Tann—Jive Brothers
Effie Green—BMG Records
Curtis Lord—Motown Records
Earline Brown—MCA Records
Martha Thomas Frye—MCA Records
Rubin—CBS Records
Bill Williams—Jive Records
Devette Singlerly—LaFace Records
Magic—Magic City
Ed Rucker—club owner
Marie Seller
Lester Pace
Marylyn Shotwell—Image Masters
Fred Smith—FedEx CEO
Kemmons Wilson—Holiday Inn CEO
LA & Babyface
Jheryl Busby—Motown Records

INTERNS

I was an intern helper for a while. I helped Kim Burse a lot. I helped Lisa McCall at the same time other interns were. Ludacris was Ryan Cameron's intern. Lil Jon was Jermaine Dupri's intern. T. I. was also with Jermaine Dupri Coco Boy at K97. Kim Burse ended up at Sony as A&R. She helped sign Destiny's Child and later became Beyoncé's road manager. Ludacris, T. I., and Lil Jon all became big stars. And now it is my time, if it's the Lord's will.

ME AND THE MEDIA

I have been so blessed to hang out with some of the biggest TV, and radio personnel. I cherish every moment.

ROBIN ROBERTS   WILL SMITH

1/60   J EWING SR.

J . EWING GALLERY
MEMPHIS , TN

William Bedford

1986 NBA DRAFT

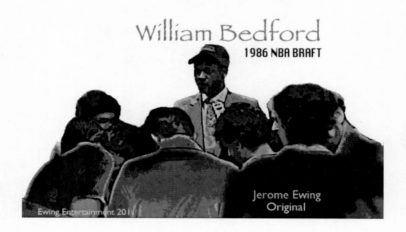

Jerome Ewing
Original

PHOTOGRAPHER
OF

THE
STARS

sought after everywere

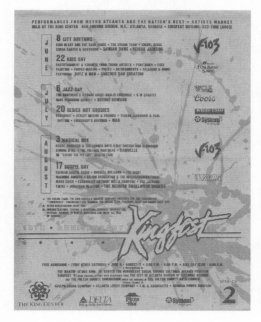

VALUE JET CRASH

This was a tough night in Atlanta. A jet took off from Miami to Atlanta and crash in the Everglades.

My business partner's, Marilyn Shotwell her husband Jarvis Shotwell and his younger brother couldn't ride together on a flight from another airline, so they switched to Value Jet just minute before takeoff.

Holyfield received a street named in his honor. A part of Old National Highway name was changed to Evander Holyfield Highway.

I covered the event for the local news papers. His dad told me he was proud of his son. I been around Holyfield many times, but this was a historic moment in his personal life.

Bobby Womack, Godfather of Soul
I would take my son with me to events that would represent a time in history.

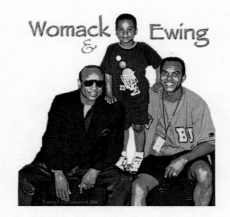

Bobby Womack

Bobby and Romey

At this time, I would be around Bobby a lot, he would play with my son all the time.

Image Masters

Marilyn J. Shotwell   C.E.O

Photo : Video

300-K Flint River Road
Jonesboro GA 30238
1 - 8 8 8 - 9 5 2 - 3 2 6 5
7 7 0 - 4 7 1 - 3 8 8 8

The Boss

Marilyn Shotwell (The Boss) and I were business partners, she was friend with my wife. Marilyn set up a photo shoot with her good friend Bobby Womack. We flew out to California to shoot Bobby, Marilyn got sick, we took her to emergency room. The next morning before my flight, me and Bobby rode to Richard Pryor's house, and he showed me O. J. Simpson's house after the shoot. Bobby told me he liked me so much because when he came, they picked us up at the airport. I ran into Jheryl Busby, who was head of Motown Records and MCA Records, and he stopped to talk to me, but it was Lisa McCall who was at Jheryl's right that I saw, and so we all talked at the airport.

As we were leaving the airport, Bobby kept saying, "You with me if Jheryl Busby stops to talk to you."

When we went to Bobby's house, he ran out to get something. About an hour later, he came back with a corned beef sandwich and said, "You said you are from Chicago, so try this."

I was blown away, first, that he remember where I was from, then, he bought us sandwiches, to make my son and I feel welcomed. When it was time for us to leave, Bobby wanted us to stay couple more days, which we couldn't. Every time I saw Bobby, he always greeted me with loving kindness.

The Jerome Ewing—The Real Mccoy

You could say I was being in the right places at the right times, or you could say that I am lucky, or you could say I am the real McCoy.

It's a little-known fact once, a producer of a major motion picture stopped the camera to give me a close-up. The movie was *The Real McCoy*, starring Kim Basinger and Val Kilmer; the producer is Lou Stroller. That was part of a magical journey. I went on from the late '70s through the '90s. The journey starts with a family destined to move from Kankakee, Illinois, to Memphis, Tennessee. One of my neighbors was Gene "Bowlegs" Miller, a legendary trumpet player for Etta James, with drummer Maurice White, who went on to start his own band, Earth, Wind & Fire. Bowlegs's love men's softball, which led him to my door. I was a cocky twenty-year-old kid who could dominate a game. Legs (as we called him) would make sure to pick me up for the game, they called me his son.

Through Legs, I got a taste of how the music business worked, what was good, and what the pitfalls were. This planted the seed, and I grew from there. It was the peak of the disco era. I would step out in the hottest spots. Once I noticed how the ladies were all over a photographer named Pier, so somewhere between him and Bowlegs was where Jerome Ewing emerged from.

I was enrolled at LeMoyne-Owen College. I took a course in photography and failed the class. Yes, I said I failed the class. The reason I failed, I didn't read the requirements. I was required to bring a 35 mm camera to class, but I didn't have one. I did what any proud fool would do. I went and bought a 35 mm camera. Then I took photography again. I fell in love with it. I soon met a staff named Jane Fleming, secretary for Lemoyne Owen College who invited me to shoot a fashion show, she was in. I met owner Odell Tidwell and Robert Mckesson. (Car Tire), who was stage manager for the Bar-Kays. I built a nice portfolio of stars like Bar-Kays, the Temptations, Stevie Wonder, and Jesse Jackson. At that time, Jesse Jackson was running for President of the United States. Remember the slogan,

Run, Jesse, Run!" president run. Kurtis Blow, Commodores, Kool & the Gang, Rick James, the Mary Jane Girls, among others? Well, by the time that I decided to move to Atlanta, my portfolio was in good shape. Little did I know that was just a stepping-stone to the big things ahead. I was on an excursion that included an impressive list of celebrities, like Michael Jackson and the Jackson family, Will Smith, Bobby Womack, Ice Cube, Jay-Z, P. Diddy, Alicia Keys, Usher, Jermaine Dupri, Luther Vandross, and Vanessa Williams. I met sportsmen, legends, singers, actors, politicians, you name them, I probably have met them.

I left Atlanta and moved back to Memphis with the idea that I would someday write a book and share my story with the rest of the world. So many of our legends are dying, so I figure now is the time for me to share a collection of my behind-the-scenes photos and the facts, that I met many of them on a personal level. So, world, are you ready for the real McCoy?

MONEY

I used to think that everybody had the same things. Then I started thinking some people have more money than others. Some people living in the city were poor, and the ones living in the suburbs, they were rich. At some point, I realized that everybody was different. My family was really different, because my mother wasn't about the money. According to her, money was to be spent and to help someone in need. My mother would find a way to say yes, if someone needed anything, like a dress, suits, if they needed to have their car fixed, food whatever they may have need of. If a friend needed something and if she thought it was important, if she did not have it, my mother would borrow the money. I remember a time I needed some money to buy a car. I could only come up with half. My mother borrowed and paid the other half. She wouldn't allow me to pay her back, she never owned a car herself. My mother never thought about herself very much. I inherited her Spirit of giving. I give of myself, my money, my time, whatever I could. God lets us know, it is more blessed to give than to receive. What I am trying to say. If you want a true blessing, then go help someone who is unable to return the favor. As a result, money has not been a driving force for what I have done in my life. Thank you mom, for the legacy you leave behind.

TELL IT LIKE IT IS

Got a call, Danny Glover, Harry Belafonte, Congress Woman Barbara Lee, serving California 13th district and, other partners would be visiting community centers in the Atlanta area. I was told I could come and take pictures. This was one of my most humbling experiences. Danny Glover really cared about the less fortunate.

KEMMONS WILSON, CEO
OF HOLIDAY INN

I was at work on September 11, 2001, when America was attacks by terrorist. I had arrived work early than usually. When the first plane hit, I got on the phone called Odell Tidwell, who was my manager at Wilson World Hotel. Mrs. Wilson called and cancelled her meetings. Business was really slow on Sundays. That was the only day that all the church people would come. Benjamin Hooks would bring twenty to thirty people with him. Sometimes, other pastors would bring their congregations. Mr. Wilson was there every week to get his ice cream. My job was to make sure that the ice-cream machine was still working. That week it went down. Odell panicked, had me run to the store, buy some ice cream put it in a bowl, just as if it had come from the machine. As soon as Mr. Wilson put the ice cream in his mouth, he knew that it was not from his ice cream machine.

He immediately asked, "Where is Odell?"

After A few minutes, he cooled off. Later we got the ice cream machine fixed, and all was well at Wilsonville. He really loved ice cream!

Then Mrs. Wilson fell and broke her hip, and that seemed to have taken the life out of the place. Mr. Wilson didn't come around every Sunday anymore. It was an honor for me just to wait on him. He took a picture with me one day, and he didn't like taking pictures. I lost the picture, and now all I have is the memory of being one of his last waiters. Mr. Wilson died shortly after that, and the hotel was sold, and all of us lost our jobs. I think just being around millionaires, you hope some of the blessing will just rub off on you.

Other notables: Lou Stroller, the executive producer of *Scarface*,

Jheryl Busby, CEO of Motown Records after Barry Gordy,

Marilyn Shotwell, my business partner (her husband was killed on the Value Jet crash in mid-'90s)

Amy Bolton, who worked at FedEx with me. (Amy bought her own video EQ, met Tyler Perry, started shooting his plays, and quit FedEx. I'm sure that she is a millionaire by now.)

Norm Stapler, who was another person who worked at FedEx with me. (He got a job with Oprah Winfrey in the early '90s.)

Ewing Entertainment Collection

The Commodores, Kurtis Blow, Kool and the Gang, Rev. Jesse Jackson, the Mary Jane Girls, the Temptations, Stevie Wonder, Prince, Sheila E., Gene "Bowlegs" Miller, Roger Troutman and Zapp, Charlie Wilson and the Gap Band, Smokey Robinson, Gladys Knight, Eddie Kendricks, Guy, Bobby Brown, Whitney Houston, New Edition, Heavy D and Boyz, Stephanie Mills, Keith Sweat, Frankie Beverly, Will Smith, Robin Roberts, Stacy Lattisaw, Jean Carnes, Al B. Sure!, Taylor Dayne, Pebbles, Toni Braxton, Lisa Lisa, LA and Babyface, Damien Dame, Jermaine Jackson, the Good Girls, Elton John, Sade, Russell Simmons, Bo Jackson, Dan Marino, Evander Holyfield, Tommy Hearns, Sugar Ray Leonard, Joe Frazier, Milli Vanilli, the 5th Ward Boyz, Cherri, Alexander O'Neal, Isaac Hayes, Johnnie Taylor, William Bell, Carla Thomas, Al Green, Alicia Keys, Jermaine Dupri, Yolanda Adams, Ice Cube, P. Diddy, Jay-Z, M. C. Hammer, Tony! Toni! Toné!, Cheryl Pepsii Riley, Gerald Alston, Luther Vandross, Vanessa Williams, Peabo Bryson, Dominique Wilkins, John Battle, Cliff Livingston, Tamar, Lisa Reye, D'brat, 112, Jagged Edge, Tiny Lister, Kid 'n Play, Martin Lawrence, Zhane, Dexter King, Lil Jon, Too Short, Ja Rule, LL Cool J, Jennifer Holiday, Chris Cross, Usher, Bobby Womack, Marvin Sease, Marvin Sapp, R. Kelly, Gregory Hines, Gino Vannelli, MC Trouble, Gerald Levert, Boyz II Men, Karen White, Tom Joyner, Jack the Rapper, Robin Thicke, OMG Girlz, Mindless Behavior, Lyfe Behavior, Three 6 Mafia, Willie Hutch, Sheba Potts-Wright, Troop, Michael Jackson, Norman Brown, Harry Belafonte, Denzel Washington, Miki Howard, Regina Bell, Tress, Angela Winbush, John Salley, TLC, SWV, and ZZ Top. Among others.

MY LORD!

If you have read my story, you can see why I believe in the Lord and why I live with the Lord on the inside of me. From the moment I can remember, a voice has been burning inside me. It talks to me daily. My consciousness is my guide. That's why material things didn't matter to me. I didn't go to church that much. Yet, I feel like church has always been in me. Sometimes I feel like I'm an angel, and sometimes I need help from an angel.

My story is full of examples of interventions. Growing up in Chicago, I thought that I was going to die more than once. The first time I can remember was going to a store on Racine Street behind Jacob A. Riis School. It was summer, and school was out. That store was on the boarder line. Blacks were living on one side, and Latinos were living on the other side. I had just moved over there at the beginning of the school year. We would go get candy from the store on our way to school, and back home. I remember walking home slowly eating my candy. As I got closer to the school (which was closed), I could see two gangs: the Blacks and the Latinos were talking. There were about ten brothers, and there were about twenty Latinos. All of a sudden, Walter (a brother) punch Deago (a Latino) in the jaw, and he went down within seconds. Everybody was hitting everybody. Bottles, rocks, including bricks, were flying. The Latinos were retreating backward. I was caught right in the middle of the Latino guys. One of them ran upon me with a baseball bat and raced up to hit me. I put my hand up to cover my face and closed my eyes, and for some reason, he never did hit me. He just ran away with the rest of them. I still thank the Lord for that, even to this day.

After all of what happened in the summer of 1972, a few weeks later, I joined a small gang or, I would say, a clique. Old Town Boys' Club was next door to my house. During the summer, some Chicago Bulls basketball players would play summer league games. Bob Love would play there. The person that took him there name was Buck. He was also the coach for the Boys' Club team. When I started going there, I became one of the best baseball player and softball player. I was also one of the best Ping-Pong players. I won MVP for softball two years in a row. I won Boy of the Year once. I won a trophy in Ping-Pong. I never thought I couldn't play basketball. However, the basketball coach didn't like me. He wouldn't allow me to play on the team, so I became a bully. I would beat up players that were on the team. I would beat up anybody that was smaller than I was. One day the best three players on the team were very early. Bing and Earl were in the gym, practicing. I left the game room because I heard the ball bouncing. I went in, and Earl and Bing were on one end, playing one-on-one. Clarence was shooting by himself, so I went down there to shoot with him. He was trying to be tough, and he told me not to shoot on his end but to go to the other end. And I said, "Fuck you!" (I had just started cursing.) I got his rebound and shot it. He started talking shit. He told me not to shoot it anymore. I stayed under the basket, and he hit about three or four in a row, and every time he threw the ball, I threw it back to him. Then he missed, and I got the rebound and went up for a layup, and that motherfucker grabbed me. He slammed me into the wall, and it was on. He was left-handed. I had never fought a lefty. We danced until Earl and Bing broke it up. They started talking shit to him and saying that I was getting the best of him. Earl asked me my name and told me I could play, and we became cool. Bing would do whatever Earl told him to do, and Clarence wasn't even from the West Side of Chicago. He was from the Southside. He would stay over at Earl's house when they had a game. When Buck found out that Clarence and I had gotten into a fight in the gym, he barred me out of there. Clarence was his star player. Those three used to hang out together every day. Now we were the Four Horsemen. Even though I couldn't go into the gym, I was running everything else. I was king of the game room and softball. We all left together every day. We would stop at a liquor store, and I would go in and get wine every night. I was only fifteen years old, but I had a beard, and I could get White Port and Kool-Aid.

One day I went to get the wine, and I was looking for Earl. When I finally found him, lying on a bench in front of Jane Addams upset. Earl was one of the toughest people that I knew. Something had to be really wrong with him. I found out that his grandmother had died. She lived with him, she was the rock of the family. We drank wine, and we were drunk, he decided he was going over to his sister's house. Her name was Yoyo, and she was a thug/gangster. She lived in the Sixteen Stories, which was a tough project that was run by gang members. There was only one way in and one way out. I had never been in there. Though we would fight them from time to time. Even when I went to Jew Town, I would go the long way around, even though it was a shortcut to go through there. Lolo's boyfriend, whose name was Big Al, was a drug dealer, pimp, and player. So Earl was feeling that he wanted to go and be with his sister. You know, you need to follow your instinct. This was one of those times for me. I had just gotten my left ear pierced, and I knew that the brothers in the Sixteen Stories had their right ears pierced. That was all that I could think about. That building was so bad, they threw someone off the twelfth floor. The police couldn't go in there unless they were in full force. As we got to the building, I didn't see anybody. I thought that maybe we could get in and get out before anybody would know. We got on the elevator, and when we got off, there was a bunch of brothers hanging around her door. They spoke to Earl, and we went on in. It seemed to me, while we were inside, a bunch of thugs was waiting for us to come out. I ain't going to lie. I was getting worried! I asked Yoyo where Big Al was, and she said he was in the building somewhere.

Now I couldn't act like I was not scared, but when Earl said "Let's go!" I started talking to my Lord, "God, I am in your hands now."

As we were leaving Yoyo's house, Earl grabbed a golf club and walked with it like it was a walking cane. I didn't have anything in my hand. So here we go. It seemed like time had stopped, and Earl would call me, "White boy, let's go!"

We were walking to get on the elevator, and some of them were walking and talking to Earl. One of them started talking smack. Earl wasn't hearing that; however, I was. It took forever for the elevator to get up to us.

One of them said, "Y'all probably need to take the stairs."

We were on the sixth or seventh floor, we waited. Somebody asked for a joint, and Earl said he didn't have one. Then he asked me for one, and I said I didn't have one either. All of a sudden, the elevator opened, and we went in. It took a minute for the door to close, and out of nowhere, a hand stopped the door. It was big Al. Damn, what a relief for me; his workers backed off. He rode down with us and walked us all the way to Racine Street. I felt like I had dodged a bullet.

I never went back in that building, even though I had met a girl who lived in there. We talked on the phone, but I moved from Chicago shortly after that. I still thank the Lord for that. I was chased by the police and had to jump out of the second-floor window. I was robbed at Crane High School, and I had a gun pulled on me on the basketball court. So when it was time for me to leave Chicago, I think it was the right move for me. I haven't spoken with any of my friends in thirty-five years. Yes, the Lord is real. If you don't believe it, reread my whole story. God bless you!

Thank You!

My Lord and Savior will always be the first and most important thing in my life. Then I thank my mother and my father for putting me on this planet. Now there have been so many angels that I have met along my journey. I would like to start with the great teachers from the first through the eighth grade. I would like to thank my teachers and friends at Saint Anne High.

My uncle Milton is gone but will never be forgotten.

Aunt Doris, Yolanda, Beverly, and April, thanks for everything. I love you!

To Aunt Be Be, Ed, Gerald, and Steven, I love you!

Aunt Lenora, I love you.

To Uncle Joe, Aunt Katie and family, thanks for making our life in Memphis so special.

To my LeMoyne-Owen College family, I learned so much, and you prepared me for what was going to come, and I hope I can someday give back to you.

Thank you to Odell and Peggy Tidwell for all the years of friendship.

To Uncle Gene and Aunt Tookie, I love you.

To Terri and the Garner family, thank you for allowing me to be a part of your family.

Julanda Robertson (Kizzy) and Jerome Ewing Jr. (Romey), you are my blood. I love you so much. I hope your future will be brighter and richer—y'all deserve more.

Courtney, I wish I could have spent more time with you. My doors will always be open to you.

To my kids, known and unknown, I have and I will always have time to listen to you and will always have something to share with you. Just pick up the phone and call me. I love you all.

To my sister Jeanine, I love you so much. You have done an amazing job raising your kid by yourself. And Gregg and Melissa have done a great job raising their kid. I love you all.

To Ed, my baby brother, stay encouraged. You have great kids, and they are taking such good care of you. I will always be there for you. Love you!

To all the talented people I have had the pleasure of working with, starting with William Bedford. We went from being just cool to now being the best of Friends. You are the real deal. Thanks for everything.

To Lisa McCall, you made my time at Motown so memorable. I love you like my sister. Thank you so much!

To Martha Faye Thomas, I will always look to you as another mother to me. Thank you so much for trusting me with all the talents that came through your door.

K. T. Karen Tann of BMG Records, thank you for all the hookup with Effaye Green and the Big Wheels at Jive Records and so on.

To Tony Scott, Curtis Lord, Bill Williams, Devert Singletary, Kenneth Frye, Janet Burley, Earleen Brown, Candice Bonner, Kim Burse (my little sister), and all the people I had the joy of working with. I hope that I wasn't a pain in the ———.

To my crew at Discovering Memphis—Sheba Potts-Wright, Candice Higgins, Derrick Baines, Drew and Que—we rocked the Memphis airways for five years, and we met a lot of people. I am proud of you all. I love each and every one of you.

Ms. Austin and Mrs. Beverly, thanks for the help with the typing of this book.

To Lula Stewart, my sweetheart, you have stopped me in my tracks and put me on a corner of prosperity and renewed my faith. Thanks for your honesty, wit and being firm with me when I really need it. You have a great family! I love them all, I know you been a blessing in my life.

Thank you for all the extra things you do. I know you were put in my life to move me into a new direction, to take me to the next level. So let's get started. I love you so much!

To all of you I didn't mention in book one I will mention you in book two. The return to Memphis, the TV show, the ups and downs. Find out which doors open and which doors close. There's so much more to talk about, so tell a friend or a book club member, and visit the website for the dates of the book signings. Until we meet again. Love you all!

Jerome Ewing
eestudio.je@gmail.com

Index

Edwards Brothers Malloy
Thorofare, NJ USA
February 10, 2015